"A sales organization is the critical interface between a firm and its market, and its strategic significance is increasing. Salespeople must be capable of understanding, dealing with, and sharing information in order to give their firm a distinct competitive advantage."

"This book provides important insights about the challenges all European sales organizations are facing as they struggle to find new ways to compete successfully. Sales directors, managers, and salespeople will find that its lucid pragmatism enables them to tackle the complexity of tomorrow's business world."
MICHELLE BERGADAA—Sales and Marketing Strategy Chair, Professor, *ESSEC Ecole Superieure de Sciences Economique (Graduate School of Economics), France*

"With 20 years of field experience as a salesperson and manager, I can say that this book is full of important ideas for anyone who wants to be a successful sales professional."
ACHIM KRAATZ—*Sales Director, Aiwa, Germany*

"At last, here is a book on selling that takes a step-function move away from the tired, traditional approach. It is a superb read, to boot."

"As author of 28 books, I can honestly say that this is a book I wish I had written myself."

"It is a superb treatment of contemporary issues including relationship management, consultative selling, retention strategies, salespeople as orchestrators and the like."

"My advice to any sales organization is to buy it, read it, and use it because it is extremely practical."
PROFESSOR MALCOLM MCDONALD—*Cranfield School of Management, England*

"In a business era where 'long-term customer relationship' is almost a cliche, the authors have succeeded in presenting a meaningful, implementable, road map for sales leaders seeking competitive advantage. This wonderful book gave me sales strategies, principles, and best practices that I will apply within my sales organization immediately."

"This is a fantastic book. My copy is already dog-eared and marked-up, and I have been quoting it in communications to my sales teams."
KEITH HAWK—Vice President, Sales—*Business Information Services, Mead Data Central*

"The smartest companies are abandoning old-style sales but not the basics of selling."

"In order to be successful in today's sales environment, companies must shape value-added services to meet the needs of the individual customer. This dynamic book outlines a straightforward process that salespeople can implement."

"This book will benefit our sales force and our customers, and will be part of our sales training process."
DIANA BOMAR—Vice President, Sales & Marketing, *Right-O-Way Transportation, Inc.*

"This book identifies the key issues facing sales organizations today, and provides the foundation for the sales team and the total organization to be successful in the global marketplace."

"To develop a successful sales organization and meet ever-changing market trends, we must challenge existing paradigms. This book is an excellent foundation to create and maintain a 'customer first' mindset not just in the sales team but the total organization. A 'must read' for the business leader of today and tomorrow."
JOHN G. O'NEILL—Vice President, Imaging, *Information and Public Affairs, 3M Canada Inc.*

"This book provided me with strategies and tactical plans to turn salespeople into account managers, and become a world-class sales organization."

"I love the checklists."
MARTIN H. HYDELL—Vice President, Marketing & Sales, *Mead Fine Paper Division*

"This book brings marketing into the 21st century. Customer retention is far different from customer loyalty, and building that loyalty through relationship management is critical in any competitive environment. The concepts stressed in this book will be useful to virtually every marketing and sales organization."
MICHAEL W. YACKIRA—Senior Vice President, Market and Regulatory Services, *Florida Power & Light*

"As businesses in all competitive markets are challenged by ever-increasing demands for higher productivity and compression of cycle times, re-engineering and aggressive revitalization of the sales process can provide a strategic advantage. This book isolates the areas of opportunity for creating a benchmark quality sales organization."

"The quality, professionalism, knowledge, and capabilities of a sales organization are the critical factors in shaping successful long-term business relationships and partnerships between suppliers and customers. In fact, the sales professional of the 90's must be prepared to adapt to ever-changing market conditions. The ideas in this book support the development of world-class sales and marketing organizations."
DR. DONALD E. LAVOIE—Vice President and General Manager, *TRW Business Credit Services*

"The creation of sales relationships is a process that must be continually enhanced to ensure the future success of every company. *High Performance Sales Organizations* will help our sales organization to achieve true success—customer delight—and creatively propel us into the year 2000."
STEVE HEPPNER—Vice President Marketing & Sales, *Dynacraft International*

"*High Performance Sales Organizations* provides new ideas, insight, and a 'road map' approach toward the solution selling that is needed in all organizations having an international presence."
PETER J. KAUFMANN—Senior Vice President, Marketing Division, *Comdisco Inc.*

"Customers today are more sophisticated in their decision-making processes, which creates new pressures on our sales force. The practical knowledge of highly successful sales organizations described in this book provides an excellent road map for success."

"*High Performance Sales Organizations* takes the mystery out of the new marketplace by introducing proven methods for achieving and *repeating* success in sales. It redefines the customer relationship in a way that can help us all—company and customers alike—to better achieve our goals."
MARY NICOL LUCAS—Director of Marketing and Sales, *Cort Furniture Rental*

"The book does for benchmarking of the sales relationship what Deming did for benchmarking the manufacturing process. It will be a standard for our salespeople and General Managers."
MICHAEL M. DICKENS—President, *Hospitality Partners*

"*High Performance Sales Organizations* is a superb guide for moving the customer relationship from 'social' to 'professional.' Sales organizations that engineer this change will become industry leaders by being greater contributors to their customers."

"Creating and sustaining competitive distinction in products and services is challenging in its own right. *High Performance Sales Organizations* is the map to effectively communicating those distinctions through a professional sales force."

"*High Performance Sales Organizations* presents some wonderful insights and great ideas for managing the 'Customer Relationship Process.' "

High Performance Sales Organizations is persuasive. In an age when keeping a competitive advantage for a sustained time is difficult, the sales force is an important distinction. The supplier who has a sales team that has moved from 'social' to 'professional' will prevail."
DAVID GUINN—Vice President of Marketing, *BT Office Products*

HIGH PERFORMANCE SALES ORGANIZATIONS

HIGH PERFORMANCE SALES ORGANIZATIONS
Achieving Competitive Advantage in the Global Marketplace

Kevin J. Corcoran

Laura K. Petersen

Daniel B. Baitch

Mark F. Barrett

IRWIN
Professional Publishing

Chicago • Bogotá • Boston • Buenos Aires • Caracas
London • Madrid • Mexico City • Sydney • Toronto

This publication is designed to provide accurate and authoritative information in regard to the subject matter covered. It is sold with the understanding that neither the author or the publisher is engaged in rendering legal, accounting, or other professional service. If legal advice or other expert assistance is required, the services of a competent professional person should be sought.

From a Declaration of Principles jointly adopted by a Committee of the American Bar Association and a Committee of Publishers.

Editor-in-chief: Jeffrey A. Krames
Marketing manager: J. D. Kinney
Project editor: Beth Yates
Production supervisor: Lara Feinberg
Designer: Mercedes Santos
Manager, graphics and desktop services: Kim Meriwether
Compositor: Wm. C. Brown Communications, Inc.
Typeface: 11/13 Palatino
Printer: Quebecor/Fairfield

Library of Congress Cataloging-in-Publication Data

High performance sales organizations : achieving competitive advantage in the global marketplace / Kevin J. Corcoran . . . [et al.].

     p.   cm.

     ISBN 0-7863-0352-2

     1. Sales management.   2. Selling.   3. Customer relations.

I. Corcoran, Kevin (Kevin J.)

HF5438.4.H54   1995

658. 8'1—dc20   94–34929

Printed in the United States of America

1 2 3 4 5 6 7 8 9   QF   2 1 0 9 8 7 6 5

Preface

Sales vice presidents and directors in every industry today are grappling with rapidly changing market forces and competitive moves. They are challenging themselves to find new answers to this question:

"How can I develop long-term relationships with my customers and improve my profitability at the same time—in a fiercely competitive market?"

If you're asking yourself this question about your own sales operation, you're in good company. Not long ago, we all focused on products and on making customers aware of product features and benefits. Today, we're focused on retaining customers, providing service, developing niche positions, and reducing cycle times. We're all struggling to anticipate the changes that lie around the bend. We all want to get ahead of the curve.

One of the frustrations is that customer loyalty is a moving target. Customers' needs are changing faster than ever. Customers also have a broader range of options available to them: There are more and better competitors in the field, running faster and working harder.

FINDING THE ANSWERS

This book will provide you with practical ideas to improve the performance of your sales organization and your business relationships with customers. We've highlighted innovative ideas, provocative points of view, and best practices that sales operations around the world are using to differentiate themselves from their competition.

These ideas are drawn from our experiences with sales and service organizations that sell primarily to other businesses in North America, Europe, and the Pacific Rim, as well as our ongoing research on customer loyalty, sales leadership, and service excellence.

Many concepts in the book reflect findings from Learning International's landmark study on global sales leadership. This research was based on the premise that a knowledge of what the leading sales organizations are doing now will help each of us to be more successful in the business environment of tomorrow. Although we heard hundreds of points of view about how sales is changing, there is one thing that everyone seems to agree on: The changes taking place in today's marketplace are affecting every aspect of selling.[1]

As a result of the research, we identified these strategies, principles, and practices that contribute to the success of leading sales organizations:

1. *A shared responsibility for asking the right questions.* In these organizations, each person—from the sales vice president to the field sales manager to the salesperson—is asking these questions:

"How are our customers changing?"

"How are our competitors changing?"

"How does our sales force add value for our customers?"

"How can we use our sales force to differentiate us from our competitors?"

These organizations believe that their ability to increase customer loyalty, competitive differentiation, and sales performance depends on a shared commitment to asking—and answering—these questions. They know that sales are everybody's business.

2. *A sales strategy based on achieving competitive differentiation.* A company's strategy for success may be based on achieving product leadership, operational excellence, or customer intimacy.[2] The sales organization, in turn, should have a sales strategy that describes its role in adding value, building customer loyalty, and differentiating from competitors' sales organizations.

An effective sales strategy is based on the answers to the questions listed above.

3. *Solid strategy and excellent execution.* Executives in many of the leading sales organizations emphasize the importance of a

---

[1]For more information on this study, see Appendix A.

[2]Michael Treacy and Fred Wiersema, "Customer Intimacy and Other Value Disciplines," *Harvard Business Review,* (January–February 1993), pp. 84–93.

dual focus on strategy and execution. They acknowledge that the success of any strategy is limited by the quality of its execution; even a brilliant strategy is useless without the ability to execute it on a daily basis, in front of customers.

A few leading-edge organizations are experimenting with a methodology we refer to as "Customer Relationship Process." This is a tool to evaluate the sales strategy, assess the alignment of strategy and execution, define best practices, set priorities, and communicate throughout an organization. Others are using this as a tool to re-engineer their sales, service, and marketing organizations to be more responsive to customer requirements and expectations.

In addition, many leading organizations have created integrated training and coaching plans that are clearly linked to sales strategy. They recognize that the ability of salespeople, and others throughout the organization, to develop relationships with customers depends on mastering the skills, knowledge, and attitudes that are relevant for today's market conditions.

THE COURAGE TO ACT

The research discussed in this book shows that the leading sales organizations are facing the same challenges that we all face. What distinguishes them is that they are aggressively questioning the assumptions on which they operate, focusing on finding the best solutions, and committing to make change happen.

We've selected the strategies, principles, and best practices that your sales organization can begin to apply immediately to help you to create a more profitable and sustainable advantage. Some of these concepts have been discussed at conferences and in corporate hallways for years. We believe the examples here will add depth to your understanding of ideas that may be familiar already.

At Learning International, we believe that the sales organizations that are facing these challenges today will be the market leaders of tomorrow.

Edward Del Gaizo, Ph.D. **David J. Erdman**
Director of Research   President and Chief Executive Officer
Learning International, Inc. Learning International, Inc.

About Learning International

Since its pioneering work in sales training in the 1960s—first as Basic Systems, then as Xerox Learning Systems—Learning International has been helping organizations succeed by strengthening their ability to build mutually beneficial business relationships with their customers. Today, Learning International is the worldwide leader in sales and service training and is a part of Times Mirror, a $3.7 billion media and information company.

Based in Stamford, Connecticut, Learning International offers an unparalleled roster of training programs and complete customization capabilities. The company conducts research on critical business issues as part of its ongoing commitment to helping clients better understand and respond to complex market changes.

High Performance Sales Organizations is drawn from Learning International's extensive sales research, more than 35 years' experience working with sales as well as organizations around the globe.

The company serves its clients through a network of offices in 28 countries on six continents.

Acknowledgments

Learning International's research studies and experiences with thousands of sales organizations around the world provide the underlying ideas for this book. We appreciate these sales organization's candor about the issues they face, as well as their willingness to share their ideas with others. We especially want to thank the 24 sales organizations that opened their doors when we invited them to participate in our global Sales Leadership research and the 11 sales organizations in Belgium and The Netherlands who participated in the pilot phase of this research. Vice presidents and sales directors, training directors, field managers and salespeople—and customers of these organizations—invested considerable time and shared valuable information with us about their strategies and operations. These companies are described in Appendix A.

Ed Del Gaizo designed and directed the research studies that are the foundation of this book and also of many of Learning International's training and development programs. In this role, he has helped to define the major challenges that sales and customer service organizations are facing today and to identify opportunities to improve their performance.

Mark ter Haar managed the Sales Leadership research project in Europe; He shared our vision, added breadth of perspective, and kept us focused on the global market. Shigetaka Takeuchi, Hideo Yamanan, and their team at Fuji Xerox Learning Institute managed the Sales Leadership research in Japan and provided many ideas that shaped our thinking.

This project would not have been possible without the extraordinary dedication of Derwin Fox, Steve Kiernan, Alexa Klimas, Kate Murray, Grace Schipani, Cindy Weissman, and Pandora Wojick. Jim King and Angela Suter deserve special recognition for their outstanding contributions. Jeffrey Krames, the editor in chief at Irwin Professional Publishing, was a constant source of enthusiasm and encouragement, as were Beth Yates and J. D. Kinney.

The efforts of Leslie Aitken, Gina Budde, Andrea Glanz, Catherine Glassanos, Steve Harker, Jaclyn Jeffrey, Jackie Malen,

John Rovens, Megan St. John, Judy Steele, and Carlos Quintero were also very helpful. Mark Jenkins of Cranfield University in England, Hans Möllfors of Zug, Switzerland, and Claude Kohly and Linda Norman of Times Mirror Training Group added a European perspective.

Finally, we want to recognize the time and talents of these contributors, reviewers, and friends, as well as dozens of other people who provided advice and support: Caren Ambrose, Margaret DeMartino, Dave Erdman, Wendy Farrington, John Franco, Helen Frith, Richard Geller, Bob Glaser, Marcia Heath, Gene Hunt, Deborah Jones, Howard Karmens, Barbara Kelly, Shelley Kramer, Jean Lambert, Dick Lucier, Clay McDaniel, Mandy Moodie, Dennis Murphy, Bob Myrstad, Susan Nelson, Karen Pacent, Barbara Palmer, Linda Pohle, Lynn Porsche, Pam Reisfeld, Cindy Renzo, Chris Rice, Clem Russo, Lou Porter, David Richards, Kathleen Richards, Betts Silver, Margery Stein, Judy Szuets, Doug Trapasso, Ron Scorsene, Gale Ulrich, David Wakefield, Michelle Wilson, and Research International, Inc.

These people helped to identify the concepts, strategies, and practices in this book with a common goal of contributing to the professionalism and performance of sales organizations around the world.

Contents

Collaborative Coaching: Farewell to the Autocratic Manager, 117

Contemporary Coaching: Overcoming the Generation Gap, 122

Breaking Down the Barriers, 124

Training for Collaborative and Contemporary Coaching, 127

Conclusion, 129

Best Practices and Guiding Principles, 130

"The concept of the 'ideal person' sought by modern society has changed from one who is a 'walking encyclopedia' to one who is prepared to solve problems. It can be said that the value of human beings rests on their creativity and ability to solve problems. It is this ability to solve problems, and solve them cooperatively, that is the key to the long-term survival of a business enterprise."

—Katsuya Hosotani, Committee Chairman, The JUSE Problem Solving Research Group, Union of Japanese Scientists and Engineers (Japan)

I

MARKET DYNAMICS

"I expect a salesperson to be a professional businessperson who happens to be involved in selling."

Chapter One

In Pursuit of Customer Loyalty

"If you have a strong relationship with a salesperson, you can live through the pricing problems, you can live through the delivery problems, you can live through anything—as long as you can trust each other."

—Customer, 3M (United Kingdom)

- What are the differences between loyal customers and satisfied customers?
- Are the differences important?
- What do customers expect from sales organizations?
- Are sales organizations meeting the most important expectations of their customers?

Faced with demanding customers and aggressive competitors, sales executives around the world confront this question everyday: "What can we do to improve customer loyalty and our own profitability in a fiercely competitive market?"

Leading sales executives say that long-term relationships are critical to the success of their organizations. In fact, nearly every one of the thousands of sales organizations Learning International has worked with in the past several years has emphasized the importance of customer loyalty.

Why is customer loyalty so important? First, because loyal customers are an important source of referrals. In addition, long-term relationships are more profitable for most sales organizations because of the costs associated with starting up a business relationship. We've known intuitively that this was true for a long time. Until recently, there was very little evidence to prove the case. That evidence is now mounting. Fredrick Reichheld and W. Earl Sasser, for example, show that a 5 percent increase in customer retention can yield anywhere between a 20 to 100 percent increase in profitability.[1]

A survey of U.S. sales organizations jointly conducted by *Sales & Marketing Management* magazine and Personnel Corporation of America in 1990 confirmed the importance of long-term relationships.[2] It suggested that profit margins from new accounts are often much lower than those for subsequent sales. In fact, it took an average of seven sales calls to close a first sale to a new customer; in contrast, it took only three calls to close a subsequent sale with an *existing* customer.

This finding is even more important in light of the increasing cost of sales calls. The same study concluded that the average cost of a business-to-business sales call was increasing at an alarming annualized rate of more than 11 percent. This means that the differential between the cost of calls to new and existing customers (33 percent in 1990) was expanding.

Long-term relationships generally may be more profitable, but the "profit" can't be taken for granted. By making too many concessions to long-term customers, or by erroneously assuming that long-term customers are also loyal customers, a sales organization can end up with solid, long-term but extremely unprofitable relationships.

The challenge that sales executives face everyday is how to make trade-offs between the two goals—how to invest in developing long-term customer relationships while achieving today's targets for profitability.

A MISUNDERSTOOD NOTION

Achieving customer loyalty is a job that's never done. Because customers are continually changing, the factors on which they evaluate sales organizations are changing also. And the bar is

---

[1]Fredrick F. Reichheld and W. Earl Sasser, Jr., "Zero Defections: Quality Comes to Service," *Harvard Business Review*, September–October 1990.

[2]William A. O'Connell and William Keenan, Jr., "The Shape of Things to Come," *Sales & Marketing Management*, January 1990, p. 38.

Loyal Customer

A buyer who chooses to do business with a particular supplier and intends to buy from that supplier in the future.

Satisfied Customer

A buyer who buys from a particular supplier, but expects to buy from others in the future.

---

continually being raised: their expectations are continually going up. Today's added value is tomorrow's expected value.

That's one reason we're all still striving for customer loyalty, after years of focusing on customer satisfaction, enhancing quality, streamlining processes, and getting closer to customers. One only has to look at the big three U.S. long-distance providers—AT&T, Sprint, and MCI—for an example. As products and services become harder to distinguish, a customer who is satisfied with one supplier in the morning can be snatched away by another by the end of the same business day. Customer loyalty is elusive: it is a valiant objective, but not a permanent state.

One reason is that the speed of product innovation and time to market is increasing. And some companies are competing with businesses that are outside their industry. Union Pacific Railroad, for example, has to compete not only with other rail transporters but also with those outside their business, including barge services and trucking companies.

Another reason that customer loyalty is hard to sustain is because it is difficult to know whether a customer is really loyal or merely satisfied. Sales organizations often assume that a repeat customer is a loyal customer. In fact, on closer examination, he or she may only be a satisfied customer—and susceptible to offers from the competition of better prices and more value.

It is important to distinguish between **loyal customers** and **satisfied customers.** Why? Because the sales organizations that succeed in the future will be the ones that segment their markets and have strategies for meeting the needs of each segment profitably. The investments they make—in resources, services, time, and concessions—to achieve their goals with each will be deliberate decisions made in the context of those strategies and with a focus on their own profitability.

THE QUEST FOR PROFITABLE CUSTOMER RELATIONSHIPS

Presumably, all organizations would like to ensure that their sales-people satisfy customers and build profitable business relationships with them—"a profitable working relationship characterized by a 'win-win' approach," as a sales manager from Boehme Chemie (Germany) described it. But not only is it unfortunate to lose the right customers, it is a mistake to *keep* the wrong customers. As most of us know, trying to satisfy *every* customer request is becoming both more expensive and painfully unprofitable.

Also, the assumption that customer retention is always profitable is just as inaccurate. Christopher Fay of Juran Institute points out, "Simply retaining a customer in no way ensures, or even heightens, the customer's loyalty." He cites an example of a computer hardware company that boasted of retaining its customer base only to find, on closer examination, that one reason its profits were not soaring was that more than half of its "loyal" customers had gone on to purchase add-ons and services from the competition.[3]

Sales executives and directors know how important profitability is, but salespeople frequently don't think about whether or not they're developing *profitable* customer relationships. Usually, their primary concern is to bring in revenue. This is understandable, given that their compensation is often based solely on meeting revenue targets. As shown in Learning International's 1990 sales force study, about half (52 percent) the sales executives interviewed said that their sales forces' goals are based simply on revenues, without taking profits into consideration.[4]

---

[3]Christopher Fay, "Royalties from Loyalties," *Journal of Business Strategy* 15, no. 2 (March/April 1994), pp. 47–51.

[4]Learning International, "Sales Productivity in the 1990s," Preliminary Report, 1990, p. 9.

Consider IBM's sales force. Until 1994, the computer giant paid its salespeople on straight commission. Now, as part of IBM's painful reorganization, salespeople will be compensated partly on the basis of customer satisfaction. According to the new compensation plan, as much as 60 percent of an IBM salesperson's commission will be tied to the profitability of each deal.[5]

BEST PRACTICES FROM GLOBAL SALES LEADERS

Learning International decided that if anyone *did* have clues about developing a profitable customer relationship, it would be today's leading sales organizations. We developed a research study to profile them and selected 24 sales leaders around the world. (See Appendix A.) Each is highly regarded within its market and industry and offers strong products and services, leading-edge research, and efficient operations. These assets certainly contribute to their customers' loyalty. Yet, these organizations have another idea about what it takes to stay competitive. What these organizations have in common is that they are challenging themselves to define what their salespeople will have to do differently to differentiate their organizations through the quality and durability of the relationships they build with their customers.

"When products and services are virtually identical, the differentiator is the salesperson and his or her management of the customer relationship," observed the vice president for marketing at American Airlines (United States).

The leading sales organizations we studied have demonstrated that they have what it takes to succeed today, and what they say about succeeding in the future is this: Success will belong to those organizations that ensure that their salespeople build lasting *business relationships* with their customers. The keys to this are building credibility, knowing what their customers want, and meeting—or exceeding—their expectations.

---

[5]Ira Sager, "The Few, The True, The Blue," *Business Week*, May 30, 1994, p. 126.

GREAT EXPECTATIONS

What is it that customers expect from suppliers? In a series of studies on customer loyalty, Learning International examined the key factors that influence a customer's decision to stay with a supplier. Business-to-business customers from a wide variety of industries in 13 countries were surveyed. Each customer was asked to provide ratings to indicate the extent to which each of 63 statements *should* describe their suppliers.[6] Participants were also asked to rate the extent to which the statements *actually* describe a current supplier. Comparisons between "should" and "actual" ratings revealed unmet, met, and exceeded expectations.

The study suggested that the six expectations listed in Table 1–1 rank highest in three major world markets—North America, Europe, and Japan.

This list of top expectations strikes at some very basic aspects of doing business. That might be predictable. But notice that five of the expectations depend on either the *salesperson's* actual performance or the expectations that he or she creates about the supplier organization and its products or services. This is very revealing. What was profoundly startling was that in all three markets most of these key expectations are unmet (see Table 1–2). Specifically:

- In North America, three of these expectations were met, but not exceeded, by suppliers: a salesperson's honesty, product and service quality, and an organization that can be trusted.
- In Europe, only one expectation was met: an organization that can be trusted.
- In Japan, supplier performance falls short of customers' expectations in all areas.

Presumably, a supplier's ability, and a customer's willingness, to develop a strong relationship depends largely on how well the supplier satisfies the customer's most basic expectations. For instance, a supplier who doesn't deliver a product on time shouldn't expect a customer to look to him to address higher level needs,

---

[6]Learning International, *Profiles in Customer Loyalty* (1989) and *Achieving Customer Loyalty in Europe* (1992). For a complete listing of the expectations analyzed in the Customer Loyalty Research, see Appendix C.

TABLE 1–1
Highest Expectations in North America, Europe, and Japan

A supplier organization that can be trusted
A salesperson who is honest
A salesperson who keeps promises
A product or service that is delivered on time
A product or service that is consistent in quality
A product or service that performs as anticipated

TABLE 1–2
Are Highest Expectations Being Met?

Expectations that Rank High in North America, Europe, and Japan	Unmet, Met, and Exceeded Expectations		
	North America	Europe	Japan
A supplier organization that can be trusted	Met	Met	Unmet
A salesperson who is honest	Met	Unmet	Unmet
A salesperson who keeps promises	Unmet	Unmet	Unmet
A product or service that is delivered on time	Unmet	Unmet	Unmet
A product or service that is consistent in quality	Met	Unmet	Unmet
A product or service that performs as anticipated	Unmet	Unmet	Unmet

such as problem-solving assistance. On the other hand, a supplier that consistently meets these basic needs has the freedom to differentiate through other, less conventional offerings. (See Figure 1–1.)

So what does the customer want? In the long run, everything. But what the customer wants now depends on what satisfaction level is currently being met. By meeting these customer needs sequentially and cumulatively, ultimately you give the customer everything, and become a partner on the inside, rather than a suitor on the outside.[7]

---

[7]Mike Herrington, "What Does a Customer Want?" *Across the Board*, April 1993, The Conference Board.

FIGURE 1–1
Hierarchy of Customer Expectations

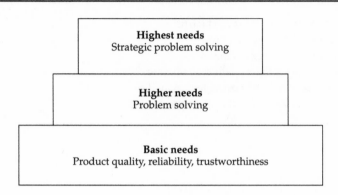

Yet, the results of the research strongly suggest that many organizations have difficulty meeting even customers' most important expectations. (See Tables 1–1 and 1–2.) Given this finding, it
is not surprising that so many companies find it extraordinarily
difficult to turn the ideal of profitable customer relationships
into a reality. Most are still grappling with the basics—making
promises they can fulfill; delivering a consistent, quality product
on time; demonstrating integrity; and establishing trust. It ap-
pears that any sales organization that is serious about competing
virtually anywhere in the industrialized world must focus on
these basic expectations.

START AT THE BEGINNING

All indications point to the sales organization's role in achieving
more enduring, more profitable business relationships as increasingly important. But where do you start?

- Look at your customer base. Identify those who are loyal
  customers and those who fall in other categories.
- Focus on improving your relationships with those who have
  the potential to become profitable, long-term customers.

- Understand how your customers are changing and how your sales force is changing. After all, the changes you make in your sales organization should ultimately link back to your customers.

- Search for best practices from other companies, starting with companies that have distinguished themselves in their own markets. Look across boundaries, into areas you may not have previously considered.

When we interviewed sales leaders and their customers in North America, Europe, and the Pacific Rim, we found that what they have in common is that they are focusing on understanding, and working with, a new type of customer and developing their salespeople's ability to sell in a consultative manner.

Chapter Two

A New Type of Customer

"If you think your relationship with the customer is nothing but a matter of buying and selling, that relationship will go nowhere. The relationship develops from additional activities that go beyond buying and selling."

—Salesperson, Fuji Xerox Co. (Japan)

- How are today's customers different?
- What do customers expect of salespeople?
- How are customer-supplier relationships evolving?
- What kind of strategy can build profitable business relationships?

You see it in the faces of your salespeople after long days on the road, and you see it in their performance. They're struggling to keep pace with a new type of customer. Not long ago, customers might have been satisfied with a fair price and a good quality product. Today, they demand a host of additional attributes—convenience of purchase, electronic data interface, after-sale support, and customization services, to name a few. Not long ago, customers could have been swayed by the salesperson's affability and social skills. Today, they are more influenced by the salesperson's professionalism and business acumen.

What do these new customers look like? What is causing them to be so much more demanding?

1. *Today's customers are more knowledgeable.* The past years' slow economic growth and the reductions in force, downsizing, and re-engineering that have "flattened" numerous organizations mean that many customers stay

in their jobs longer than in the past. As a result, many of them are more knowledgeable about what they are buying and how their decisions relate to their organization's needs. A vice president at Bayerische Vereinsbank Group (Germany) commented on the typical customer's expanded base of knowledge, "Customers are more self-confident, and they know how to make use of their knowledge."

2. *Today's customers are more analytical.* Customers' buying decisions are more closely linked with key business strategies and require difficult choices about how best to use their organizations' limited resources. "Customers are very tough right now," said a sales manager for Xerox Corporation (United States). "They are more educated about business problems and the effect of their buying decisions on their P&Ls." Big-ticket or complex purchase decisions receive the most intense scrutiny, especially from high-level executives. Customers must be thoroughly analytical about all their purchase decisions, basing them solidly on the strengths of the supplier organizations' solutions.

3. *Today's customers are more demanding.* To respond to increased competition in their own markets, today's customers juggle more responsibilities with fewer resources and must, therefore, operate more efficiently and effectively. Because customers are pressed to do more with less, they are more determined than ever before to get good value for their investments. "My expectations are simple," commented a customer of Ordo (France). "I want the best possible service." Customers have a strong sense of entitlement, the result of the many options available to them as more suppliers compete for their business. As a salesperson for American Airlines (United States) said, "The travel agents who are my customers are dealing with 12 or 15 of my competitors. They won't put all their eggs in one basket." Said a sales manager from Rank Xerox (The Netherlands), "Clients have better insight about their options." The result? Customers' expectations have soared. "We're expected to do it all, at lower cost," reported a vice president of Hewlett Packard Company (United States).

4. *Today's customers provide more strategic information.* Today's customers expect more, but they are also willing to give more. In the interest of making the best purchase decisions

for their organizations, more customers—especially in North America—are willing to share substantial information with the salespeople with whom they work.[1] As a vice president at Xerox Corporation (United States) observed, "There has been a major change in customers in that they are much more open in dealing with salespeople." As a result, sales conversations are more candid, and, as a salesperson at Allen & Hanbury's (United Kingdom) noted, "Customers have a more positive attitude toward selling." Said a sales manager from Scott Paper Company (United States), "Salespeople and customers used to think of themselves as on opposite sides of the desk—as adversaries. Now there's more respect—more trust. We work together to develop the customer's business."

This increase in the information that is shared between suppliers and customers symbolizes a radical change in business relationships at the most fundamental level. It reflects a new level of trust and a new type of partnership.

CUSTOMERS' EXPECTATIONS OF SALESPEOPLE

"An ideal salesperson has a deep knowledge about his or her product and can recommend the best solution for a specific customer."

—Customer, Tokio Marine & Fire Insurance Company (Japan)

As markets become more competitive and customers become more sophisticated, customers have *higher expectations of the salespeople with whom they do business.* They expect their suppliers' salespeople to recommend solutions that will be focused on helping them compete more effectively. A sales manager with Iron Trades Insurance Group (United Kingdom) summed up the new expectation this way: "Customers are buying a concept as well as a product. They are looking for value for their money—and someone to make their business more profitable."

---

[1]Learning International's white paper, *Achieving Customer Loyalty in Europe* (1992), shows that customer-supplier relationships appear to be at various stages of development, due to different political, economic, social, cultural, and competitive factors. For example, the four customer attributes just described are most noticeable in the North American marketplace and less so in Europe and Japan. As the European and Japanese markets become more open, supplier organizations are experiencing increasingly similar competitive pressures and escalating customer expectations.

Equally important, they expect salespeople to exhibit the same high level of business knowledge and sophistication that they do. In the words of a vice president at Océ (The Netherlands), "The customer's expertise is growing, and he or she expects to work with a salesperson who can be considered an equal." A customer of Scott Paper Company (United States) put it this way: "The level of competence demanded of salespeople will take quantum leaps. They need to be more clever, more professional, and have more technical knowledge because the customer base is more sophisticated about business." In addition, customers expect salespeople to perform the time-honored, customer-focused sales practices more often and more consistently.

Three areas of knowledge are essential for salespeople today:

1. *Comprehensive knowledge of the customer's industry, company, and strategies.* Salespeople in all world markets today are expected to be familiar with the customer's industry and the impact of new global competitors. Particularly in North America, salespeople are also expected to provide insight into how their product can support the corporate strategies their customers deploy, from implementing total quality to reducing the supplier base. As a customer of Scott Paper Company (United States) described it, he values salespeople who focus not just on his needs but also on those of his customers—i.e., on the customer's customer: "What's unique about Scott's salespeople is that we work in partnership with them to reach the end user. They always keep in mind that the ultimate customer is the end user. This is different from most of their competitors, who think of the distributor as the ultimate customer."

2. *In-depth knowledge of their own company's full range of product and service applications . . . and the products and services their competition offers.* Downsizing, re-engineering, and outsourcing have also produced greater "information expectations" among customers. As a salesperson for Scott Paper Company (United States) noted, "Customers don't have time to become experts in what I sell, so they rely on me to have the expertise." Customers base their decisions not only on how well a product meets their needs but also on how all the related services that supplier organizations

offer can support their strategy and help them compete.[2]
Customers expect the salesperson's expertise to extend to
competitive products as well. According to a salesperson from
Ordo (France), "Customers don't want to work with
salespeople who know only their own products. Salespeople
also have to know the products and services offered by
competitors." Some customers expect even more. A customer
of Rank Xerox in Sweden, for example, singled out that
company's salespeople because they were "better at
cooperating with other suppliers to find the complete
solution." Hewlett Packard (United States) has told its
salespeople that they must not only be knowledgeable about
their own products but also complementary products from its
many partners.

3. *A thorough understanding of general business management.*
   Customers expect the salespeople they work with to have
   the critical business judgment and expertise necessary to *use*
   the strategic information given them. Said a customer of
   Scott Paper Company (United States), "A good salesperson
   can answer the question, 'If we decide to do business with
   you, how will our business grow?' I always ask salespeople
   this question, but I rarely get an answer." As a salesperson
   from Rank Xerox (The Netherlands) put it, "A client expects
   you to think with him about his business, his alternatives,
   and what the return would be for each alternative chosen."
   In some customer organizations, this expectation may have
   grown out of the decision to use fewer suppliers, which
   creates the need for a greater sense of partnership, or trust,
   between the customer and its suppliers.

In addition, customers say that one of the most significant factors influencing the supplier's ability to meet their expectations is
the tenure of the salesperson in the sales assignment. Customers
put a high value on working with salespeople who know the customer's organization intimately. Further, they resent the time required to orient a supplier's new salesperson to their business.[3]

---

[2]For their part, salespeople view this expanded demand as an opportunity to practice
some healthy protectionism. As a salesperson at Scott Paper Company put it, "We look at
an account on the basis of the services we can offer to protect our position."

[3]Importantly, customers of the companies in our research frequently volunteered this
point, yet few of the sales organizations brought it up.

Xerox Corporation (United States) recognizes this critical need and has developed a program to assign senior managers to selected accounts, with the specific goal of providing continuity and a consistent presence for the customer. Of course, this approach has many other benefits as well, not the least of which is what senior managers learn as a result of having direct customer contact.

So, what is the reward for equipping salespeople with high levels of knowledge and business savvy—and the skill needed to apply it? Customers tend to view salespeople who meet their expectations as a *resource*—as people who can help them meet their goals, educate and inform them, solve business problems over the long term, and meet the needs of their internal and external customers. In short, the reward is customer *loyalty*. As a customer of Ordo (France) put it, "The more competent the salespeople are, the more I rely on that company."

THE EVOLUTION IN PROFESSIONAL RELATIONSHIPS

"Golf games and friendships don't guarantee customer loyalty anymore. It's the performance that counts."

—Salesperson, Scott Paper Company (United States)

Strong customer relationships are built on rapport, trust, and respect between the salesperson and the customer. In the past, many salespeople focused on developing these qualities on a personal level as a way to differentiate themselves. This was a successful and accepted strategy. As a sales manager from Union Pacific Railroad (United States) put it, "Before deregulation, when most prices were the same, selling was a matter of building a social relationship. You took customers out to lunch or dinner, and, if they liked you, you got the business."

Today, developing business through social skills is still important, but it's not enough. Its success depends too much on the compatibility of the personalities involved. If a salesperson should accept another position, or, for whatever reason, relinquish control of the account, the sales organization is highly vulnerable to losing the business entirely.

Furthermore, customers can no longer rationalize the choice between two suppliers on the basis of friendship. They must justify
the choice on the basis of *business* factors. For example, a study of
buyers in the electric utility industry found that credibility, reliability, and responsiveness were the most highly rated salesperson
competencies and that "degree of initiative taken" was considered
more important than friendship in making a sale.[4]

Certainly rapport, trust, and respect on a personal level are still
important. But today, business relationships are based less on personal small talk and more on the salesperson's ability to address
the customer's business concerns. Trust comes less through the
salesperson's persuasiveness and charm and more from his or her
ability to substantiate—through actual performance—the truth of
his or her claims.

THE ULTIMATE CHALLENGE: DEFINING A SALES STRATEGY

"The keys to success will be increased productivity of our sales force, mea-
surement of the sales process, feedback from customers that drives continuous
process improvement, and identification of alternate distribution channels for
different segments of our business."

—Vice president, Hewlett Packard Company (United States)

Many leading sales organizations have defined a sales strategy
that will differentiate them through the strength of their
salespeople's business performance with customers. They believe this strategy will give them a sustainable, competitively
distinct advantage in a demanding, unpredictable business
environment.

The sales leaders that Learning International studied are
focused on the one thing they have a great deal of control over
and that their competition will find it most difficult to copy—
that is, the quality and durability of the relationship between
their organization and their customers. This is true at both the
micro level (salesperson to customer contact) and the macro

---

[4]Hayes and S.W. Harley, "How Buyers View Industrial Salespeople," *Industrial*
Marketing Management 18 (1989), pp. 73–80.

Northwestern Mutual Life Insurance Company:
"Sociable Professionalism"

Northwestern Mutual Life Insurance Company's (United States) approach to building trust and rapport with customers is a reflection of the transition from social to professional business relationships.

During their sales calls to prospective customers, Northwestern Mutual's agents use a survey form called the FactFinder, which contains questions about a client's assets, liabilities, monthly expenses, investments, insurance coverage, and other financial details.

Agents work with the customers to complete the form in a conversational style using questioning skills and listening skills. The agent also responds empathetically to the personal information shared. This approach is designed to accomplish two objectives: to identify the client's needs and to build the relationship. By the time the FactFinder is completed, a sense of trust and rapport has been created and the foundation for a solid business relationship is built.

level (organization to organization). These organizations are working to establish an **ideal business relationship** with every customer with whom they choose to do business.

Each of them is using a different array of concepts, practices, and tactics to achieve this goal: team selling, sales force automation, re-engineering, and continuous improvement are among them. As you will read in the following chapters, some are familiar approaches but these organizations have applied them with a unique structure, discipline, or focus. In any case, all of these leading organizations are committed to flawlessly executing their strategies, because they've learned that the success of any strategy is determined largely by the quality of its execution.

Managing, tracking, and improving all the factors by which the sales organization develops customer relationships is a daunting task. One Learning International study showed that to ensure that a sales force achieves its goals for both customer satisfaction and profitability, sales management may need to monitor at least 45 separate activities ranging from "ensuring that sales managers regularly coach and give feedback to salespeople" to "forecasting

> **Ideal Business Relationship**
>
> A business relationship characterized by a sense of rapport, trust, and respect between the salesperson and customer, with the expectation that their organizations will do business over the long term and in a mutually beneficial way.

sales accurately."[5] To bring order and priority to the task, several of the leading sales organizations that Learning International studied are applying the principles of business process management to their business relationship–building efforts. Their pioneering work, described in the following chapter, will set a new standard for sales excellence and performance.

BEST PRACTICES AND GUIDING PRINCIPLES

- Ensure that your customer satisfaction measurement system assesses what customers in three major world markets said was most important:
  - Salespeople who are honest; salespeople who keep promises.
  - Products and services that are delivered on time, perform as anticipated, and are consistent in quality.
  - A supplier organization that can be trusted.
- Ensure that the people in your sales organization have a common understanding and share a common vision in the following areas. Ask yourself:
  - What are the dynamics of our market?
    - What is our customer profile?
    - How are our customers changing?
    - What are our customers' expectations of our sales force? How are these expectations changing?
    - What is influencing those changes?
    - How are our competitors changing?
  - What is our sales strategy?

---

[5]Learning International, *Sales Productivity Action Planning Guide* (1992).

- How will our sales strategy help us to differentiate from our competition? Build profits, and stay competitive? Improve customer satisfaction?
- What are our competitors' sales strategies?
- How does our sales organization add value?
    - What value does our sales force add for our customers, beyond that which our products or services provide? What value *could* they add?
    - How do our competitors' sales forces add value for their customers?
- What are our sales priorities?
    - What priority do our salespeople give these three goals: revenue, profits, customer satisfaction? What priority do our sales managers give them?

II

BUILDING CUSTOMER RELATIONSHIPS

"A good salesperson can answer this question for every customer: 'If we decide to work together, how will the customer's business grow?' "

Chapter Three

The Customer Relationship Process

"For continuous process improvement, you have to have in place a model and all the measures and tools to know how you are performing at any moment. Then you have to keep pushing the model to get more productivity out of it, to get higher quality from the sales process, and to get more customer satisfaction at the other end. You may be very comfortable with your model, and it may even be a breakthrough. But others will be watching you and seeking ways to improve it. You cannot rest on your laurels."

—Vice president, Hewlett Packard Company (United States)

- How do quality management principles apply to sales organizations?
- What is a Customer Relationship Process? What does it look like? How can it help your company become more competitive?
- What is the role of salespeople in ensuring the success of the Customer Relationship Process?
- What is the value in mapping your Customer Relationship Process?

As we discussed in the first two chapters, today's leading sales organizations are determined to differentiate themselves through the strength of their relationships with their customers. A few organizations have found a tool to help them describe the ideal customer relationship. They have created a map to help them focus on the activities that truly make a difference to customers—and to avoid wasting resources and time on misdirected efforts.

These organizations—including Xerox Corporation, Scott Paper Company, and Hewlett Packard Company in North America and Avis Fleet Services in Europe—have introduced the principles of quality management to the sales organization. Quality principles have helped these pioneering sales organizations better define and communicate their priorities to their salespeople and their customers, re-engineer and restructure to better meet customers' needs, and formulate and execute powerful, competitively distinct strategies for building stronger customer relationships.

Though these ideas are logical and simple, they are revolutionary for a sales organization—a functional area that has long been characterized by entrepreneurial spirit, fierce individualism, and an aversion to detailed analysis and measurement. Yet, they are producing powerful answers to the fundamental question that plagues every top sales executive: how to improve both sales performance and customer satisfaction—profitably. This chapter looks at how some of the pioneers of the "quality in sales" movement are putting their ideas into practice.

INTRODUCING QUALITY PRINCIPLES TO THE SALES ORGANIZATION

"The quality initiative over the last few years has focused us on satisfying a customer's total requirements."

—Vice president, Xerox Corporation (United States)

Total quality management (TQM)—whose principles, processes, and rigorous methods were once confined to the manufacturing plant—has found its way into almost every functional area in organizations and industries of every description. Its leaders (W. Edwards Deming, Joseph M. Juran, Philip Crosby, David Garvin, Armand Feigenbaum, and Genichi Taguchi, to name some of the most prominent ones) have schooled an entire generation. This approach defines quality in terms of customers' needs, recognizes the tie between quality and profitability, includes quality planning in the strategic planning process, and stresses continuous improvement organizationwide. Typically, the goal of quality management is to analyze, streamline, and perfect the organization's business processes so that the organization can meet or exceed customers' expectations at the least cost.

Companies throughout the industrialized world have embraced total quality management—and with good reason. "We've found that businesses labeled 'high quality' by their customers are two to three times more profitable than businesses ranked lowest on the quality scale," observed Devereaux Dion, senior vice president of the Strategic Planning Institute (SPI), a Cambridge, Massachusetts, not-for-profit research organization.[1] SPI bases its conclusion on cumulative data from its Profit Impact of Market Strategy (PIMS) database, which includes financial, marketing, and competitive information on 3,000 participating business units.

It is certainly easiest for supplier organizations to view and analyze their business processes from their own vantage point. However, to gain a clear understanding of the activities that influence customer satisfaction, it is critical to examine the business processes from the customer's point of view. For example, sales organizations have traditionally defined their activities as a sales cycle. With the new emphasis on customers, some organizations have instead begun to try to focus themselves on the **Customer Relationship Process (CRP).**

The Customer Relationship Process is, literally, what the *customer* experiences when interacting with a supplier organization's people. It consists of the entire sequence of person-to-person business encounters—regardless of functional area—that comprise the customer's full experience with the supplier organization. Most of these encounters occur with the organization's front-line sales and service professionals. In fact, some organizations define their Customer Relationship Process as the combination of the sales cycle and the service cycle.

What is immediately apparent is that every business, from the one-person shop to the multibillion dollar corporation, has a process for working with customers, that is, a Customer Relationship Process. Most organizations, however, have never defined it or analyzed it; and because they don't isolate it and critique it, they cannot manage it or improve it.

---

[1]Learning International, *Exchange* no. 36 (1991), p. 3.

Customer Relationship Process (CRP)

The sequence of activities performed by the people who are in direct contact with customers that enable the supplier organization to meet or exceed customer requirements.

Some organizations, however, are using quality principles and tools to define, study, and document their CRPs. Whether they choose to map the process using flowcharting or to describe it in detailed text, their goal is to identify the activities that will help them close the gap between customer expectations and what their organization delivers. Documenting the CRP helps these organizations uncover vast amounts of critical information that they can use to make strategically important decisions about their organization's direction, processes and procedures, hiring practices, training and coaching priorities, and rewards systems (see Figure 3–1).

Mapping an organization's CRP will help it to

- Identify and analyze its people's interactions with customers.
- Measure its people's performance against customer requirements and competitors' performance.
- Involve customers in a dialogue about how the organization can change its CRP to better meet their needs.
- Establish a common language that can be used within the organization and with customers to describe how the organization works with customers now—and how it would like to work with them in the future.
- Clarify the roles, high-value activities, and competencies required of the front-line people whose daily interactions build the customer relationship.
- Standardize and replicate the actions and behaviors that customers most value and that can differentiate the organization from its competition.
- Establish improvement priorities and allocate resources accordingly.
- Better understand—and meet—the needs of various market segments by examining the CRPs that best meet their needs.

FIGURE 3–1
The Performance Model

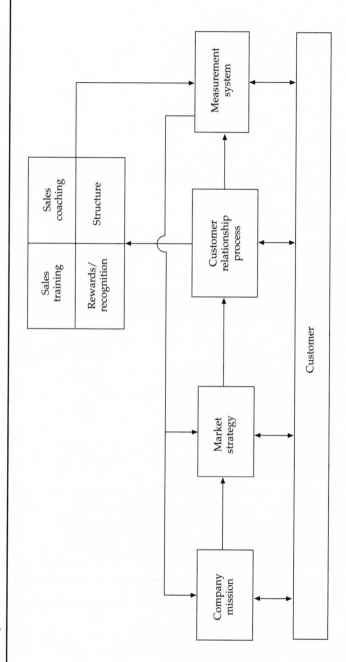

29

As Michael Porter wrote in *The Competitive Advantage of Nations,* "Competitive advantage grows out of the way firms organize and perform discrete activities . . . Firms create value for their buyers through performing these activities . . . To gain competitive advantage over its rivals, a firm must either provide comparable buyer value but perform activities more efficiently than its competitors (lower cost), or perform activities in a unique way that creates greater buyer value and commands a premium price (differentiation)."[2]

While mapping, analyzing, and improving the critical activities of the CRP cannot eliminate all the variables (e.g., a competitor's actions or a key contact moving on to a new job), following these steps can enable the supplier organization to improve the quality, speed, and accuracy of the actions it *can* control. It can help an organization identify the activities that are critical, eliminate unnecessary activities, and thereby provide a method to control or reduce the costs associated with sales and service. Continually improving the CRP increases the chances that every interaction with customers will improve the business relationship.

FOCUSING ON CRITICAL ACTIVITIES

"We have always measured sales performance in terms of end results—in terms of quota, growth, and new accounts. That may not be the best way to measure performance. We also need to look at the steps of the process and measure those. If we do well at the steps, the end results will absolutely come."

—Sales manager, Hewlett Packard Company (United States)

The organizations that are using the CRP as a framework offer this advice, adopted from the quality movement: The key to achieving cost-effective delivery of services is to focus on the few activities that are most critical to productivity and customer satisfaction. These are high-leverage activities that an organization must perform correctly to satisfy customers, and the ones that differentiate it from competition.

---

[2]Michael E. Porter, *The Competitive Advantage of Nations* (New York: The Free Press, 1990), p. 40.

Customer Relationship Process—Company X

Phase 1: Establish the relationship.

• Qualify the prospect.
• Gather information.
• Introduce capabilities.

Phase 2: Analyze the customer's requirements.

• Define the requirements.
• Clarify the buying process.
• Validate requirements.

Phase 3: Recommend solutions and gain commitment.

• Validate proposal with customer.
• Prepare a presentation.
• Gain commitment to specific recommendations.

Phase 4: Implement the recommendations.

• Initiate setup.
• Monitor installation.
• Initiate follow-up.

Phase 5: Maintain and expand the business relationship.

• Institute follow-up procedures.
• Initiate formal review of customer satisfaction.
• Identify new opportunities.

Typically, these organizations develop a user-friendly flowchart or description that condenses the complex picture of how the organization builds relationships into a handful of phases and their associated activities.

Most CRP documents start out as text that lists the phases and their activities. The example shown in the preceding box is of one organization's Customer Relationship Process.

The same CRP "mapped" as a flowchart (see Figure 3–2) portrays a snapshot of the process. The level of detail with which an organization describes its CRP phases and activities depends largely on the organization's culture, the complexity of its products and services, and the intensity and nature of its competitive challenges—although "keep it simple" is the advice of most of the pioneers who are currently using it.

The interactions between salespeople and customers figure prominently in a CRP; the data about these interactions can be used to evaluate a sales strategy. Other organizations use the CRP framework to examine their customers' experiences with the supplier organization's service people or to develop a marketing strategy. The follow-up section looks at how two organizations, Avis Fleet Services and Premier Hospital Supply, Inc.,[3] have used CRP mapping to develop and communicate strategies in two critical areas: sales and marketing.

APPLYING CRP MAPPING TO IMPROVE COMPETITIVENESS: TWO CASE STUDIES

"It forced us, as a business, to look at what we want our salespeople to do and how we want to support that with resources."

—Key accounts manager, Avis Fleet Services (Belgium)

Avis Fleet Services

Avis Fleet Services, a European business that provides car fleet leasing and related fleet management services, is a pioneer in the use of the CRP. This company has used CRP analysis to help it define and launch a new marketing strategy.

Avis Fleet Services is the largest fleet service company in Europe, operating in 27 countries. Backed by the resources of its corporate owner, GE Capital Fleet Services, the company is committed to identifying significant opportunities for growth. In 1993, its goal was to develop a new market strategy that would capitalize on a key competitive strength: its ability to

---

[3]Not this organization's real name.

FIGURE 3–2
Customer Relationship Process

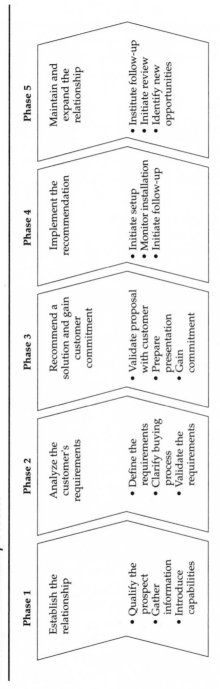

Phase 1	Phase 2	Phase 3	Phase 4	Phase 5
Establish the relationship	Analyze the customer's requirements	Recommend a solution and gain customer commitment	Implement the recommendation	Maintain and expand the relationship
• Qualify the prospect • Gather information • Introduce capabilities	• Define the requirements • Clarify buying process • Validate the requirements	• Validate proposal with customer • Prepare presentation • Gain commitment	• Initiate setup • Monitor installation • Initiate follow-up	• Institute follow-up • Initiate review • Identify new opportunities

TABLE 3–1
Customer Development Process—Avis Fleet Services

---

1. Earn the right.
   Build credibility and gain customer commitment to proceed to the next phase.
2. Share information.
   Gather and exchange information required to understand the customer's needs.
3. Develop solutions.
   Consider and exchange alternatives and design possible solutions.
4. Agree on the recommendation.
   Recommend final solution and obtain customer agreement.
5. Implement.
   Deliver products and services according to customer expectations.
6. Maintain and expand the relationship.
   Satisfy customer by fulfilling current and future needs.

Copyright © 1994, Avis Fleet Services

serve the Pan-European market as one unified company while being flexible enough to respond to the needs of local markets.

"Our original intent," said the manager of key accounts, "was to define a standard way of doing business and to find a way to describe to the sales force what we want them to communicate to customers."

The first task was to define a sales approach that would be effective in 27 countries and appropriate for the 10 company-owned operations as well as the licensees. At the same time, Avis Fleet Services needed to create a unified organization, rather than 27 powerful fiefdoms, that was capable of meeting the needs of Pan-European customers. It would not be enough to create a unified Avis promise if the organization could not consistently deliver on that promise throughout Europe.

Avis Fleet Services defined a "customer development process" that describes the critical phases of developing customer relationships throughout Europe (see Table 3–1). Avis's customers and prospects evaluate its proposals based on a lease-versus-purchase analysis, the terms and conditions, and the value-added service that Avis provides. The manager commented, "Our salespeople need to know the *best* way to show how we provide value to the customer."

The customer development process has also enabled them to see some glaring gaps in the information that some countries compile. "What's most exciting is that this has become a way to share best practices across the countries," the manager went on. "It's a way to pull the best practice of the top salesperson and share it with 200 other salespeople. In addition, this has given us a way to communicate with our management about what's going on in the field. Now, we can show them how our salespeople are going to work with the client to develop the sale and come to a close. They can see that it's not just a pitch—it's 31 separate steps."

Equipped with this clear and agreed-upon statement of what it believes about customers' needs, Avis Fleet Services now has a tool to guide its marketing strategy and a common language for communicating within the organization and with customers about what those needs are. "We certainly could have done it without mapping the process, but this has given us an organized and me-thodical way to share the information," said the manager.

Premier Hospital Supply, Inc.

Another example of a company that has used CRP mapping to im-prove its competitiveness is Premier Hospital Supply, Inc. (PHS), a medium-sized medical supply company in the United States. Pre-mier's industry is experiencing slowed growth: sales to hospitals and physicians have decreased as buyers have grown more cau-tious. Tighter controls imposed by managed care providers have translated into increased pressures for cost containment.[4] In this environment, Premier faced the challenge of reducing costs with-out reducing customer satisfaction. Because Premier is a distribu-tion company whose products can be obtained from a number of other distributors, the only way to differentiate itself from its com-petition is through the services it provides to customers.

PHS decided in 1993 that it needed to focus on those services that provided the most value for its customers. Analysis of its Customer Relationship Process was a promising way to start.

---

[4]Standard & Poor's Industry Surveys, *Health Care Products and Services* (9 September 1993), p. 39.

Premier held several two-day meetings with customers to discuss the following:

- The activities of the current Customer Relationship Process.
- What the customers perceive as PHS's strengths and weaknesses.
- What the customers recommend that PHS do differently.

The outcome of the meetings was a preliminary map of the Customer Relationship Process. The map showed six phases, each of which was broken down into distinct activities.

The PHS project team and each sales branch office reviewed the CRP map and suggested improvements. In addition, each region held focus groups with customers to obtain their feedback on the CRP. Said the leader of the CRP team, "We wanted to know what customers expected from a sales rep, from start to finish. Our map is the result of the best ideas from all those who participated."

Among the benefits PHS has seen from the CRP map are improved ability to service its customers, clearer organizational direction, more frequent and open communication with new and existing customers, and a precise focus for sales training.

In addition, the work on the CRP led to a change in the company's competitive strategy. The company believed that its needs analysis service, which it offers to customers as a way to define their priorities, was of significant value to customers, and was a competitively distinct service. In reviewing the Customer Relationship Process, PHS customers said that the needs analysis step *does*, in fact, provide value. But the customers told PHS that it does not differentiate the company because many of PHS's competitors also conduct needs analyses.

Involving customers enabled PHS to gain detailed, current information about what its customers value—and about how its competition was changing to meet those expectations. The company used this information to re-evaluate its competitive strategies and identify new ways to differentiate itself.

"We intend to continually update our Customer Relationship Process map to reflect the changing needs of our market," said the executive vice president.

STEWARDSHIP OF THE CUSTOMER RELATIONSHIP PROCESS

"In the future, the best sales managers will be sales process managers."

—Sales manager, Hewlett-Packard Company (United States)

The many sales organizations that have endorsed the CRP as a core business principle believe that salespeople must be the *stewards of the Customer Relationship Process*. The process may include people from many different functional areas within the organization, but the salesperson remains the customer's primary contact for as long as the relationship lasts.

In fact, Learning International's research on customer loyalty, discussed in Chapter One, shows that five of the six elements that determine a customer's decision to continue to do business with a supplier organization depend *either directly or indirectly on the salesperson's actions or the expectations that he or she creates about the organization*. In North America, the research showed that the salesperson's ability to influence customer loyalty is so strong that "even if customers were unhappy with some aspect of the product performance or service follow-up, the salesperson could keep the relationship intact. This was true *if* the customer felt reassured that the sales organization was ready and able to go the extra mile to restore the relationship."[5]

As the strategic orchestrator of the process, the salesperson needs to know how the CRP will unfold—not just at the sales presentation in the client's office, but also when the customer service rep answers the service call, when the billing clerk generates the invoice, and when the technical expert comes to the client's factory. Whether these people are organized as an account team or working in their own departments, the salesperson can take the initiative to coordinate their efforts.

As a vice president from Océ (The Netherlands) put it, "In the future, everything we sell will be products that are part of a system. Everything will be integrated. This implies that the salesperson has to oversee the total concept instead of just his or her

---

[5]Learning International, *Profiles in Customer Loyalty* (1989), p. 9.

part." Understanding the Customer Relationship Process helps an entire organization focus on the customers' needs; but the sales organization—and specifically, the salesperson—should be the steward of the process on behalf of the organization and its customers.

A PRACTICAL METHOD FOR CRP MAPPING

"From the beginning, we try to help a new representative to create good habits by using the well-established selling process."
—Sales manager, Northwestern Mutual Life Insurance Company
(United States)

Whether an operation defines the entire CRP or merely the subset of activities that directly involve the sales force, mapping may not be an easy task. It requires tremendous organizational commitment and discipline. Getting an organization to change on the basis of what the CRP map reveals is even more challenging—especially if the organization already believes itself to be highly successful. As a vice president from Hewlett-Packard Company (United States) commented, "The biggest challenge is answering the question, 'We are already successful; why should we change now?' "

The organizations that have documented their CRPs, including Learning International (see Figure 3–3), offer the following basic guidelines:

1. *Start with a commitment to better understand and improve how the organization relates to its customers.* The initiative must have a high-level champion, someone who believes in and understands the value of applying quality and business process management principles to the task of building customer relationships—and who has the authority to make it happen.

2. *Define the phases of the Customer Relationship Process simply and concisely.* An overly complex CRP document will be too cumbersome to use and is more likely to produce confusion than offer guidance.

3. *Anticipate the customer's expectations for each phase.* For example, the customer may expect a salesperson to have in-depth knowledge of the customer's industry.

FIGURE 3–3
The Customer Relationship Process

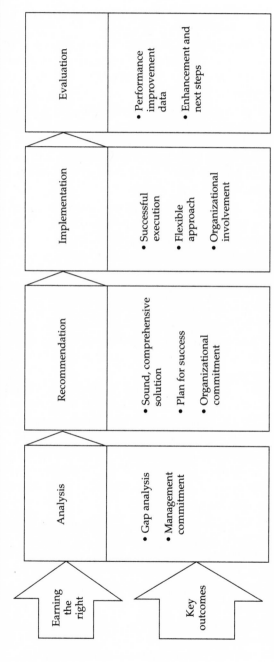

4. *Define the activities, tools, and resources needed to cost-effectively meet customers' expectations for each phase.* Identify the amount of time and resources that can be devoted to each phase.

5. *Define the performance standards that you will use to assess how well your front-line sales and service professionals meet your customers' expectations.* Most organizations are experimenting with ways to measure sales success over the long *and* short term. A new focus is on measuring sales success with respect to profitability and customer satisfaction, as well as revenue. A salesperson at Scott Paper Company notes that Scott not only measures customers' satisfaction with its products and salespeople but also "their satisfaction with our competitors."

6. *Validate the Customer Relationship Process map with customers.* Solicit customers' input to ensure the usefulness of the activities in the process and the quality of their experiences in each. This will also help ensure buy-in from the front-line sales and service people, who are far more likely to respect a process they know their customers have reviewed and approved.

7. *Gather information from customers about their current and future needs, and examine the competition's strengths and weaknesses with respect to the CRP.* The people who are face-to-face with customers everyday, particularly sales and customer service people, should be involved in analyzing this information to select improvement priorities that take into account the competition's current strengths and weaknesses.

8. *Improve selected activities.* Once the activities of the process are clearly defined, it will be far easier to set priorities for improvement, develop standards, measure and benchmark against those standards, add value, and reduce cost for the selected activities.

9. *Define best practices.* Seek out appropriate models against which to benchmark, whether from within the organization or outside of it. "We are trying to measure what the good salespeople do that the others don't," said a salesperson with 3M (United Kingdom), "to learn lessons from them and teach others."

10. *Use feedback from customers to track progress and identify additional activities to improve.* Once the organization has accepted discussion of the CRP as part of its culture, the

likelihood of continuous improvement of standard operating practices increases because of the ability to focus on specific activities and specific feedback. This is critical because of customers' continually escalating demands and today's volatile marketplace conditions.

CONCLUSION

"We now have a focus on customer satisfaction, whereas in the past, it was totally on revenue, profit, or the number of 'net adds.' "[6]

—Vice president, Xerox Corporation (United States)

The migration of the concepts and techniques of the quality movement into sales organizations has helped many operations to define their goals so that they are consistent with their customers' expectations. It has also helped bring into focus the importance of using customer satisfaction to measure the sales organization's success.

The Customer Relationship Process is another example of a core quality concept that has profound implications for sales organizations. It enables an organization to bring logic, order, and consistency to the everyday actions and behaviors of everyone who interacts with customers. It is an indispensable tool for re-engineering all the processes that touch the customer. By identifying the activities that its customers value most, a sales organization can make decisions based on the *customer's* priorities, not the organization's. When developed properly, the Customer Relationship Process helps organizations identify the activities that, when performed flawlessly, significantly improve their long-term relationships with their most important customers.

BEST PRACTICES AND GUIDING PRINCIPLES

• Map your Customer Relationship Process.
  • Conduct internal interviews, as well as customer interviews, to get a broad description of:

---

[6]"Net adds" are the number of new units sold minus the number of units replaced. Net adds represent growth over the number of units previously in use.

- The steps in the process.
- The relative value of each to the customer.
- The customer's definition of quality for each step.
- Activities that comprise each step.
- Objective evidence that the step has been completed.
- Ensure that the map outlines phases, or stages, as well as activities associated with each phase.
- After mapping the Customer Relationship Process, invite customers to comment on it to verify that it represents the way they want to buy from your organization.

Use your Customer Relationship Process.

- Identify the needs of different markets, and different market segments, as well as how your organization will meet those needs.
- Focus on the CRP in conversations with customers. Ensure that customers understand and provide input on how you will work with them, what they can expect to receive from your organization, and what expectations you can satisfy.
- Identify important competencies, as well as coaching and training needs. Coaching and training decisions should specifically address gaps between "expected" and "actual" performance, as identified in the CRP.
- Develop and enhance your competitive strategy and competitive opportunities. For instance, identify steps in the process that you perform better than your competitors, where you add value and they do not, and vice versa.
- Use customer satisfaction data to evaluate the performance of people in your sales organization.

Chapter Four

Consultative Selling

"In the future, selling will be a balance of customization and standardization. We'll have a portfolio of standard offerings and we'll be able to customize a unique solution to meet each customer's needs. This is the essence of consultative selling."

—Vice president, Scott Paper Company (United States)

- What is consultative selling?
- How does traditional selling compare with consultative selling?
- What are the elements of strategic problem solving?
- What roles does the consultative salesperson fulfill?
- Is consultative selling a worldwide trend?

The Customer Relationship Process described in Chapter Three is a powerful tool for identifying and improving the activities that establish and strengthen profitable, long-term relationships between your organization and your customers. The knowledge, skills, and attitudes your salespeople use will determine the strength of the relationship between your two organizations.

Sales executives in the leading sales organizations say that the critical skill salespeople need to develop long-term customer relationships is **consultative selling.**

The process of consultative selling enables a salesperson and a customer to gain a mutual understanding of the customer's strategic goals and to achieve them by working collaboratively. The key word is *strategic*. With these goals as the basis for the sales conversations, the salesperson and customer can create a highly focused and targeted solution together. Information flows both ways. Recommendations are based on mutual understanding and agreement.

> *Consultative Selling*
>
> The process of helping the customer achieve strategic goals through the use of your product or service.

The customer comes to view the salesperson as an ally—a trusted advisor and resource—as they work together toward the customer's strategic goal.

Today, more and more customers are eager to participate in this kind of sales process. "Customers are now disclosing much more information: They believe that it is in their best interest to be open and exchange information with our salespeople," reported a vice president at Xerox Corporation (United States). "They will tell you what the requirements are and the names of the other suppliers they are working with. This is different from the 1970s, when the tone was almost an adversarial relationship. Today's customer/supplier relationships are built on openness, candor, and trust on both sides."

STRATEGIC PROBLEM SOLVING

"The salespeople I value most are problem solvers, not proposal writers."

—Customer, Océ (The Netherlands)

Customers place a high value on salespeople who are able to help them with strategic problem solving. What a customer describes as strategic problem solving is what a sales organization thinks of as consultative selling (see Figure 4–1).

The salesperson who wants to be an effective strategic problem solver will need the skills and knowledge to be able to:

- Uncover and understand the customer's *strategic needs* by gaining an in-depth knowledge of the customer's organization.
- Develop solutions that demonstrate a *creative* approach to addressing the customer's strategic needs in the most efficient and effective manner possible.
- Arrive at a *mutually beneficial agreement*.

FIGURE 4–1
Building Customer Relationships

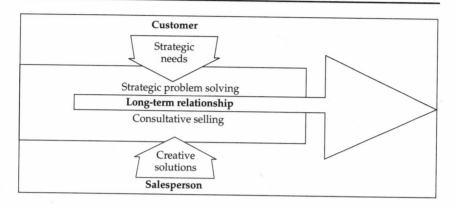

Three key terms in the preceding list—strategic needs, creative solutions, and mutually beneficial agreements—are critical to strategic problem solving.

Strategic Needs

Every customer need has a reason behind it. Usually that reason is another need, or a need behind the need, that represents a strategic goal the customer wants to accomplish.

It might help to think of the customer's range of needs as an onion. The first layer represents the need initially described by the customer. The next layer represents the reason for that initial need—the need behind the need. By peeling away the layers of each need, the salesperson eventually uncovers the core, or strategic, need. The consultative salesperson who understands the full range of the customer's needs is in a much better position to provide a product or service solution that helps the customer progress more efficiently and effectively toward achieving his or her organization's strategic goal.

For example, suppose you're a computer salesperson and one of your prospective customers expresses a need to equip her sales force with laptop computers. The traditional sales approach would be to immediately describe the features and benefits of

FIGURE 4–2
Need Behind the Need

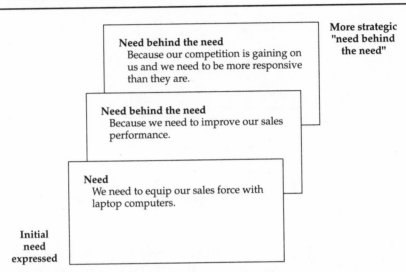

your line of laptop computers. Using a consultative selling approach, however, you would first explore the reasons the customer wants the computers. You may find, for instance, that there's a competitive issue: the customer's competition is perceived by the marketplace as more responsive. Therefore, the customer's strategic need is to be more responsive (see Figure 4–2). Having this information can help you describe the specific aspects of your product line that address the customer's need (to be more responsive) and identify other ways your company might be able to help the customer meet that need. For example, you might offer the services of your company's 24-hour help line or offer to work in partnership with another supplier to develop a customized software program for the new laptops the customer is purchasing from you.

Usually, a need behind the need falls into one of three categories:

- *Financial*—improving monetary results or controlling costs.
- *Image*—maintaining or improving prestige.
- *Performance*—maintaining or improving productivity.

Needs in these strategic areas do not exist in a vacuum; they interrelate and influence each other. That's why top-performing salespeople make sure their probing strategy covers all three areas. As noted earlier, only by understanding and addressing the full scope of the customer's needs can the salesperson recommend a more comprehensive, long-term solution. When this happens, the salesperson gains not only the customer's increased level of trust and respect, but also an edge—sharpened by his or her knowledge of the customer's long-term goals—in uncovering new selling opportunities.

"The top salespeople have a breadth of vision," said one vice president at Xerox Corporation (United States). "They can figure out the customer's requirements and come up with a set of specifications that the company can deliver on to meet the requirements. And they can work through complex situations."

Creative Solutions

Each customer is faced with a specific, unique combination of strategic needs and business issues.

As a result, each customer requires a specific solution from the sales organization. The ability of a salesperson to tailor a "custom" solution for each customer is critical today. The salesperson needs to use **creative problem solving** to identify the specific solution that meets each customer's needs.

For most companies in most industries, the competitive necessity to understand and respond to the customer's more complex and strategic needs spells the end of the one-size-fits-all solution. In the past, the *product* was the solution; now, more often than not, the salesperson must create the solution from a mix of products and services. Usually, the solution represents either one of two options:

1. A *customized version or application* of a product and/or service that efficiently addresses the customer's specific strategic needs.

2. A *mix of products and services* (including, if appropriate, competitors' products and services) that offers the best possible solution in light of the customer's strategic needs.

Creative Problem Solving

The ability to develop and combine nontraditional alternatives to meet the specific needs of the customer.

The better a salesperson is at creatively marshaling all available resources to address a customer's strategic need, the stronger the customer relationship becomes. This ability to solve problems creatively is one of the characteristics of top salespeople at the leading sales organizations we studied. As a vice president at Scott Paper (United States) described them: "There's a creative energy around getting the answer."

Mutually Beneficial Agreements

Salespeople and customers say that a significant shift has occurred in their expectations of the outcome of sales agreements—from the adversarial "win-lose" to the more collaborative "win-win" arrangement. To achieve a mutually beneficial agreement, salespeople and customers must work together to develop a common understanding of the issues and challenges at hand. Then, together, they can reach a solution that makes sense for both organizations.

To ensure mutual benefit, both parties may agree that, for the time being, the best arrangement is *no* arrangement. This (hopefully) rare circumstance may arise when the salesperson's organization is unable to offer a tenable solution, or the customer's expectations are so high that the sales organization cannot respond to them profitably.

The salesperson's focus on mutually beneficial solutions creates mutual *commitment* to those solutions. This commitment, in turn, enhances the prospects of successfully implementing the solution, thereby strengthening the relationship—and the prospects of doing business together in the future.

Information about an organization's business strategies is often highly confidential. But more and more customers, in the interests of developing solutions that will help achieve their strategic goals, are willing to let salespeople cross the threshold of confidentiality. A customer's willingness or reluctance to share confidential information depends on cultural norms and on the salesperson's ability to develop trust, meet the customer's expectations, and fulfill all the roles of a consultative salesperson.

What Do Customers Want?

According to customers, the best salespeople:

• *Are committed to helping their customers succeed.* They know that, to ensure the success of a long-term relationship, they must help their customers achieve long-term objectives.

• *Stay involved with their customers,* even if there is not an immediate sales opportunity.

• *Always focus on the customer's strategic needs* when developing solutions.

AN EVOLUTION IN SELLING

"Clients have dramatically changed the way they buy. Salespeople have to adapt to this new situation; they must be advisors to clients."

—Salesperson, Biscuiterie Nantaise (France)

Recent decades have brought important changes in selling. Once, the typical sales call was a "pitch"—a presentation focused on a specific product and tightly controlled by the salesperson. Today, the best sales calls are highly interactive dialogues between a salesperson and a customer working toward a common goal.

Sales executives who are thought leaders envision the sales call of the future as a balanced exchange of information, based on trust and focused on achieving a mutually beneficial agreement. Their assumption is that the more information—and control—that's shared, the better the solution will be.

Two related developments have paralleled this one. An evolution from selling products, to selling products and services, to selling products and services and added-value services, has taken place as competitors have caused companies to look for new ways to differentiate. In addition, customer needs have become more complex and more strategic, which makes customers want to do business with sales organizations that can help them meet those needs.

Taken together, these trends represent an evolution from traditional selling to consultative selling, as described in Table 4–1.

TABLE 4–1

Comparison of Traditional and Consultative Selling

	Traditional Selling	*Consultative Selling*
Role of salesperson	"Lone ranger"	Strategic orchestrator Business consultant Long-term ally Key player in the customer's business
Involvement of customer and salesperson	Minimum customer involvement; maximum salesperson involvement	Heavy involvement of both customer and salesperson
Information flow	One-way: salesperson to customer	Two-way
Focus of interaction	Product/service features and applications	Ability of the solution to address the need behind the need—such as the customer's improved financial performance
Knowledge required	Own company's Products and services	General business and industry trends

	Competitors
	Applications
	Account strategy
	Costs
	Opportunities
		Own company's
		  Products and services
		  Competitors
		  Applications
		  Account strategy
		  Costs
		  Opportunities

		Customer's
		  Products and services
		  Competitors
		  Customers

Skills required	Face-to-face selling skills	Face-to-face selling skills, including in-depth probing
		Strategic problem-solving
		Demonstrating how solutions meet strategic objectives
		Team-building and teamwork
Salesperson's involvement in customer's decision-making process	Uninvolved Isolated from decision-making process	Involved
Salesperson's involvement after purchase and installation	Very little: "hit and run"; move on to the next customer	Salesperson continues to call on customer organization to ensure successful long-term performance
		Salesperson directs the activities of the Customer Relationship Process throughout sales and service cycles

THREE ROLES OF CONSULTATIVE SELLING

"We must take the business and sales status of each retailer into account, and guide and instruct each one concerning the additional value of each product."

—Salesperson, Shiseido Company (Japan)

The evolution from traditional selling to consultative selling requires salespeople to be more versatile, creative, and visionary than ever before.

To help sales organizations understand—and become proficient at—selling consultatively, Learning International conducted a two-phase research study designed to determine what effective and less-effective salespeople do differently.[1] The research results helped define consultative selling on a more practical level.

The first phase of the study investigated the types of behaviors that characterize the most successful salespeople. Results of this phase revealed several major findings, which were consistent across industries:

1. Effective salespeople play not one, but three, roles: strategic orchestrator, business consultant, and long-term ally.
2. The higher the ratings for all three roles, the higher a salesperson's quota achievement.
3. Salespeople who had been in their jobs for at least five years received higher overall ratings for the three roles.

These findings suggest that salespeople need to fulfill all three roles to be effective at consultative selling. (See Figure 4–3.)

The second phase of research identified specific practices associated with each of the three roles. These practices are included in the "Best Practices and Guiding Principles" sections at the end of Chapters 5, 6, and 7.

We'll examine each of these roles in detail in the following three chapters. In the meantime, the following paragraphs offer a quick overview.

In the role of **strategic orchestrator,** survey respondents said the salesperson works to harness all of his or her company's resources for the customer, seeking assistance from others and

---

[1]For an explanation of this study, see "Roles of the Salesperson" research in Appendix B.

FIGURE 4–3
Three Roles of the Consultative Salesperson

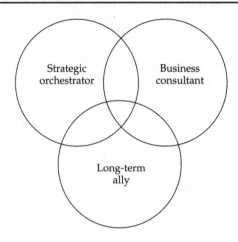

building cooperation. The salesperson involves colleagues at all levels of the organization and adopts a problem-solving approach to production, delivery implementation, and service concerns. The salesperson is also able to weigh the costs and benefits of various value-adding activities and make the customer aware of them in a way that builds the business relationship.

As an effective **business consultant,** the salesperson uses internal and external resources to gain an understanding of the customer's business and marketplace. The salesperson thoroughly educates the customer about the products he or she offers, as well as how they compare with competitors' offerings. The salesperson has well-thought-out plans for his or her territory and for each account. He or she approaches problem solving and decision making with creativity and an understanding of the "big picture."

In the role of **long-term ally,** the salesperson acts as a business partner, working to support the customer even when there is no immediate prospect for a sale. He or she positions products and services honestly and turns down business that isn't in the customer's long-term interest. The salesperson "goes to bat" for customers whenever necessary and helps customers carry out fact-finding missions within their own companies. In addition, the salesperson shows pride in his or her company, products, and services.

Consultatively Speaking

The following are selected quotes from our sales leadership research on the subject of consultative selling . . .

- "Successful people will be the ones who understand their company's strategy. This will be true for salespeople and for customers."
- "Needs-based selling will continue to evolve so that we are truly focused on the customer's business goals and total system needs."
- "We used to sell products; now we sell solutions."
- "We are pushing our salespeople to see themselves as consultants and sales professionals."
- "Our vision is for our salespeople to understand the business problems of the account, to know how to get to high levels, and to develop relationships."
- "We can help our customers look at the business in a different way. We can help them get a product to market faster by examining the steps in the process and telling them how to reduce the steps. It's a question of document flow—it's not a question of selling a copier."
- "Salespeople can help customers find new ways to solve business problems, to look further than price and features. We want the account to look at us as more than the seller of the box; we want to help them look at utilization and the bigger issues."

Many organizations have found they need to train their salespeople to recognize the value of the individual roles and the way the three roles interact to create a long-term bond with customers.

The findings of this study make a connection between the three roles and today's business realities, including the increased emphasis on service and escalating customer expectations. The research demystifies the often nebulous notion of consultative selling and creates an observable link between the three roles and quota performance. It also suggests that top sales professionals have evolved far beyond supplier status in the eyes of their customers.

CONCLUSION

Sales executives from all industries and all countries say that the ability to develop long-term relationships with their customers will be critical to the success of their business in the future—and that the ability of their salespeople to be consultative will be an essential factor in achieving this goal.

As a sales manager at Siemens (Germany) said, "Each salesperson must have an understanding of how the market has changed, so he or she can invest the appropriate activity and energy in the right place."

The term *consultative selling* is not a new one, but these sales executives are redefining it to reflect the values of today's more sophisticated customers and the abilities of today's more sophisticated sales forces.

The next three chapters describe the three roles of consultative selling. A complete understanding of each of these roles—strategic orchestrator, business consultant, and long-term ally—is critical to fulfilling this vision.

BEST PRACTICES AND GUIDING PRINCIPLES

- When gathering information, analyzing data, and recommending solutions, the focus should be on the customer's *strategic* needs—the needs behind the needs that may have been initially expressed. Key to this is a probing strategy that uncovers issues related to financial, image, or performance needs.

- Salespeople have to earn the right to be seen as consultative salespeople. Their first challenge is to build credibility. They achieve this by demonstrating integrity, reliability, and expertise.

- Customers say that sales organizations should give salespeople the authority to make important decisions independently. This allows them to meet customer needs promptly, and gain customers' trust and respect.

- Salespeople should be able to provide creative solutions to strategic problems in an efficient and effective manner. To do this, sales organizations should be set up to provide customized, nontraditional applications of products or services. Combinations of products or services, even including those of competitors, may be needed.

Chapter Five

Salesperson as Strategic Orchestrator

"In the future, salespeople will work on multifunctional teams. There won't be any more 'Lone Rangers.'"

—Vice president, Scott Paper Company (United States)

- What is a "strategic orchestrator?"
- What does the strategic orchestrator do for the customer?
- What practices and competencies are associated with the strategic orchestrator role?
- What is team selling? Why is it an example of the strategic orchestrator role?
- What leads to successful team selling?

In response to customers' escalating expectations and increasingly complex problems, successful salespeople have learned to draw on the full range of resources of their organizations. Figure 5–1 shows the three roles of the consultative salesperson. Fulfilling all three consultative roles enables salespeople to manage the information explosion that confronts them, while developing partnerships that benefit their own organizations as well as their customers'.

This chapter discusses the role of strategic orchestrator and its relationship to effective team selling. Chapters 6 and 7 will examine the other two roles of the consultative salesperson, business consultant and long-term ally.

FIGURE 5–1
Three Roles of the Consultative Salesperson

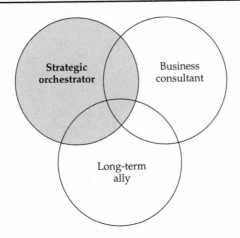

REVOLUTION IN BUSINESS RELATIONSHIPS: FROM ONE-ON-ONE TO ORGANIZATION-TO-ORGANIZATION

As customers' needs become more and more complex, many customer organizations have set up *buying teams* to ensure that their organizations accurately convey their complex needs and thoroughly assess the accuracy of suppliers' recommendations. In addition, they demand more information, ideas, and resources from sales organizations so they can address these needs and achieve their goals.

There was a time when customers were content to work with a single contact from a supplier organization. Very often, the salesperson was the *only* person from his or her organization whom the customer knew. Today, however, fewer and fewer customers are comfortable with this arrangement. Customers want access to a supplier's full range of resources. Furthermore, if they are going to share strategic information to address the ever-widening scope of their business challenges, customers want the assurance that an *organization*, not a single individual, is committed to the relationship.

Leading sales organizations are *equally* uncomfortable with having a single point of contact between the customer and their organization. Sales organizations realize that they are unable to adequately meet the customer's needs and expectations if only one person is working with the account. And if they don't meet those needs, a more responsible competitor will. They recognize that customers expect their supplier relationships to involve more than just contact between one salesperson and one buyer. In addition, there is the danger of losing the business and losing the account information and relationship if the salesperson leaves the assignment.

As business relationships evolve from one-on-one to organization-to-organization, a critical part of the salesperson's new role is to ensure that establishing and sustaining customer relationships is perceived as everyone's responsibility—not just the salesperson's.

STRATEGIC ORCHESTRATORS: STEWARDS OF THE CRP

"Our best salespeople are team captains, not individual stars."

—Sales manager, Hewlett-Packard Company (United States)

A fundamental change in the role of the salesperson is to serve as the primary contact between the two organizations and to make the customer aware of the network of resources that stands behind the salesperson. The best will assume the role of **strategic orchestrator.** Strategic orchestrators harness *all* their company's resources for their customers. They know whom to contact, and how to manage their involvement, so that they can put together unique solutions for customers or address their production, delivery, or service concerns. Observed a salesperson for Boehme Chemie (Germany), "I *manage* these accounts; I do not merely sell to them."

In their role as strategic orchestrators, salespeople are stewards of their organization's Customer Relationship Process (see Chapter Three). They make sure they are kept informed about—and have the opportunity to influence—every significant customer contact with their organization, whether at the supplier

---

Strategic Orchestrator

A salesperson who coordinates all of the information, resources, and activities needed to support customers before, during, and after the sale.

---

organization's inbound telemarketing center, field office, warehouse, customer service department, or the client's receiving dock and installation site. When appropriate, top salespeople create additional activities—and involve people from different functional areas or with different expertise or authority—to optimize the customer's experience and ensure that the organization delivers what the customer values.

As a vice president from Iron Trades Insurance Group (United Kingdom) remarked, "Linking service and sales is important to build relationships; there is no longer just one person selling the business. We are selling the whole company."

WHAT A STRATEGIC ORCHESTRATOR IS—AND DOES

The salespeople who best fulfill the role of strategic orchestrator, and therefore, sell consultatively, will, according to Learning International's research, be people who have mastered six key competencies. These competencies are:

1. Knowledge of their own company's structure.
2. Expertise in building and managing a team.
3. Ability to manage priorities and performance.
4. Ability to coordinate delivery and service to their customers
5. Efficiency.
6. Flexibility.

The specific practices associated with each of these competencies are discussed in the following paragraphs.

Northwestern Mutual Life: The Hidden Dimension of Service

At Northwestern Mutual Life Insurance Company (United States), agents frequently draw on the resources of a "hidden dimension" of the organization: the attorneys and other specialists who serve the policy owners behind the scenes, although they never meet them. These people provide advice to the selling agent about the solutions and programs the agent has designed, to ensure that they are based on sound legal and financial principles and current laws.

"What do your top agents do that is different from what your average performers do?" we asked. A sales manager responded, "Hard work, smart work, team work."

Knowledge of their own company's structure. Salespeople who fulfill the role of strategic orchestrator have a comprehensive understanding of their company's mission, markets, products, and competitors. They are familiar with their organization's policies and procedures, with how the different departments operate, and with who has the power to make key decisions. They also know who in their company communicates most effectively with clients and who is more effective "behind the scenes." As a sales training supervisor from 3M (United Kingdom) commented when asked about what it will take to succeed in selling in the future, "It's not just selling skills or relationship building that will be important. Salespeople will have to be able to manage the resources available to them." Said a customer of Tokio Marine and Fire Insurance (Japan), "The truly excellent salesperson sells by effectively utilizing internal resources."

Expertise in building and managing a team. Strategic orchestrators realize that to meet the expectations of today's customers, they need the cooperation of others within their own organization. For that reason, they develop knowledge of the organization's "political structure" and maintain good working relationships with superiors, colleagues, and support staff. They use excellent communications skills to build a team that is willing and able to meet customer needs. Their ability to manage this team throughout the selling process and beyond quite simply makes salespeople more productive. "Top salespeople know how to delegate," observed a sales manager from Northwestern Mutual Life Insurance Company (United States).

Ability to manage priorities and performance. Along with their ability to manage a team, strategic orchestrators are able to manage their own priorities to achieve continuous performance improvement. They assign a priority to every task and invest their time appropriately. They know how to establish realistic, but challenging, personal performance goals and achieve them by setting specific, short-term objectives. "Top salespeople achieve goals that are based on their own clear vision," noted an area sales manager for Sony Corporation (Japan). Because they monitor their progress, they know when there's a problem, and they can develop a specific action plan to remedy the situation. They constantly seek feedback from others on ways to improve their personal performance.

Ability to coordinate delivery and service to their customers. Strategic orchestrators are committed to their customers' satisfaction, even after a sale has been made. As a vice president from Xerox Corporation (United States) observed, "Top salespeople are concerned about total customer satisfaction and have the desire to make sure that everything is going right with the customer." To ensure customer satisfaction, strategic orchestrators coordinate all aspects of product and service delivery, making sure that the customer understands what is happening at every step. They do not limit their interactions with customers to sales calls; they maintain high visibility even when others within their company are working directly with the customer. They also determine if any additional resources are needed to serve the customer—and when, where, and how to obtain them.

Efficiency. "Strategic orchestrators spend a lot of time planning what they need to do to achieve goals so they don't waste time," said a sales manager from Iron Trades Insurance Group (United Kingdom). They maintain an efficient sales recordkeeping system, complete routine paperwork on time, and make sure their administrative activities do not interfere with customer-related tasks.

Team Selling

When a team from the supplier organization meets with a potential
or existing customer with the intention of advancing a sales cycle
and building a business relationship.

Flexibility. Effective strategic orchestrators are able to
adapt well to a wide variety of situations. They are comfortable
juggling priorities and responsibilities, selling a variety of products and services, and working under deadline pressures to meet
requests and expectations of multiple customers. As a vice president from Xerox Corporation (United States) commented can-
didly, "Top salespeople are mature enough to work through the
problems and always focus on the customer's requirements."

Customers of strategic orchestrators have a high level of confidence in the salesperson and in the salesperson's organization. As
a customer of Océ (The Netherlands) put it, "The way the salesperson mobilized his sales organization and eventually solved the
problem left me feeling, 'With this guy, I can do business.'" This
increased confidence can lead to faster purchase decisions, increased repeat business, and strengthened bonds between customer and supplier organizations.

Top-performing organizations recognize that the salesperson, in
the role of strategic orchestrator, can make invaluable contributions
to team-based initiatives. For example, at Union Pacific Railroad
(United States) the national account managers are the customers'
primary contacts. They coordinate the efforts of others and lead
teams from a wide range of departments to solve problems, identify quality- and satisfaction-improvement opportunities, and
strengthen the relationship between customers and Union Pacific.

Strategic orchestrators put these practices to good use in organizations both large and small—whether they orchestrate the steps
of the Customer Relationship Process across time zones or simply
across town. Sometimes, it may be appropriate for the customer to
remain unaware of the salesperson's role in coordinating people,
products, and information. At other times, the salesperson's

demonstrated ability to put an array of resources at the customer's disposal is what cements the business relationship. One of the ways that salespeople use their abilities as strategic orchestrators most visibly is through team selling.

AN EXAMPLE OF STRATEGIC ORCHESTRATION: TEAM SELLING

As discussed earlier, customers today look for salespeople and their organizations to demonstrate greater depth and breadth of knowledge about the customers' businesses. Team selling is one way to achieve this expectation by bringing resources and information—in the form of the people who are best prepared to answer the customer's questions or concerns—into an actual sales call.

It may take place over the phone, in person, or even by video teleconference. Regardless of venue, the purpose of **team selling** is to advance the sales cycle by bringing appropriate players from the supplier organization into a sales discussion with a potential or existing customer.

Team selling can differentiate the sales organization by quickly providing customers with a wide range of information, advice, ideas, and even decisions. No more "Let me get back to you on that," or "Why don't I have one of our engineers give you a call?" The supplier organization can use team selling as a mechanism for providing customers with answers quickly and efficiently.

Fuji Xerox (Japan) has used team selling for many years as a key element of its strategy to build long-term relationships with customers. The salesperson coordinates the involvement of members of the technical staff, marketing staff, and others to ensure that customers are fully informed about the capabilities and applications of the most up-to-date equipment.

Involving people with different personalities and communication styles in a sales call is particularly advantageous for addressing a wide range of issues or for reinforcing key points. As a salesperson at Allen & Hanbury's (United Kingdom) said, "One person might be able to deal more effectively with certain aspects of the call, or certain customer attitudes, and another person can deal more effectively with others. Also, it adds credibility when you are backing up each other's statements."

From the point of view of the supplier organization, the presence of several people on a sales call provides the opportunity to view the sales interaction from a variety of perspectives. The participants in a team sales call can obtain more relevant and accurate information than a lone salesperson ever could. The salesperson—or team—can then use that information to plan more efficiently and develop better strategies. The bottom-line impact is improved sales productivity.

What do customers think about team selling? They say that team selling has many advantages. It helps them:

- Ensure that their concerns are heard and their needs are met.
- Obtain a bigger picture of the products, services, and solutions that the supplier organization has to offer.
- Determine whether (or how well) the different departments of the supplier organization work together.
- Obtain customized recommendations that mesh with strategic business goals.
- Reach better and faster agreements on price, deliverables, and terms and conditions.
- Exchange vital technical and business information with their counterparts in other companies.

As a customer of Océ (The Netherlands) summed it up, "Team selling gives me the opportunity to get commitments from the people who are responsible for different activities."

Although large corporations have set many of the precedents for team selling, authors Cespedes, Doyle, and Freedman point out that it can be as useful to the three-person consulting firm as it is to the multinational conglomerate.[1] In fact, the relevance of team selling for a particular situation often has far more to do with the *customer's* needs than with the size or structure of the supplier organization. Consider three of the applications in which team selling is most effective: high-technology solutions, warehouse/superstore sales, and global solutions.

Team selling is a critical tool for organizations that market high-technology products. Constant advancements in high technology

---

[1]Frank V. Cespedes, Stephen X. Doyle, and Robert J. Freedman, "Teamwork for Today's Selling," *Harvard Business Review* (March–April 1989).

make it difficult for a single salesperson to remain up-to-date on new developments. Leading sales organizations find that teams of people can more easily satisfy customers who have complex challenges, needs, and expectations. "As you move from single products into more sophisticated systems, team selling is the only way to go: Technical support people, administrative support people, and installation people all have to work together to meet the customer's requirements," said a sales manager from Xerox Corporation (United States).

Team selling is essential to developing appropriate broadbased solutions. As a vice president from Hewlett-Packard Company (United States) observed, "The resource-intensive sale demands leaders who manage all the team members." Another reason these companies turn to team selling is because installation, service, and support have become so critical; the customer demands evidence of how both the salesperson *and* the behindthe-scenes team will service the account after the sale. Customers say that team selling is a service-oriented activity that sets a company apart from its competition.

Another type of organization that often profits from team selling is warehouse stores—operations that sell items in bulk quantities from groceries to housewares in bulk to consumers. The success of these superstores depends on their buying power, which is backed by sophisticated inventory, availability, and delivery tracking systems. Teams from the retailers expect to work with teams from supplier organizations to get better service and lower prices. The coordinated, team-sell approach is crucial, particularly in cases where suppliers sell multiple products through different sales forces.

Team selling is also important among organizations that have a growing number of multinational customers. The complex problems associated with crossing geographical and organizational boundaries, managing different currencies, and achieving multiple objectives require both savvy team leadership and intense team participation.

MAKING TEAM SELLING WORK

For all its benefits, team selling does present some formidable challenges. First among these is the issue of compensation. Unless they

---

Team Selling at Hewlett-Packard Company

Team selling is widely used now at Hewlett-Packard Company (HP) (United States), but it wasn't always this way. Until the late 1980s, HP's salespeople marketed primarily to management information systems (MIS) people, who, at the time, made the purchase decisions for their companies.

However, as their knowledge and expectations expanded, HP's clients began making buying decisions at higher levels in the organization. HP salespeople found that, although they still held the customary technical conversations with their MIS contacts, they now had to justify purchases with the client's financial representatives and explain to its executives what the technology would do for their company.

It became clear that a lone Hewlett-Packard representative could not expect to attend a sales meeting and have at his or her fingertips all the data the customer needed. To address the knowledge deficit, HP salespeople began to bring experts with them to talk about the technical details while they discussed how the proposed product applications would address the customer's specific business issues.

Over time, team selling took on form and substance. The company began to map the sales process so they could replicate it and expand upon the team selling experience. Building on the lessons they learned from their manufacturing quality initiative, HP management established customer feedback systems and developed the team selling procedures the organization uses today.

---

are compensated for their contributions, many potential members of a sales team may be unwilling to devote time and effort to helping salespeople sell. As one district sales manager bluntly put it, "I've got monthly numbers to meet with limited time and resources. I don't get paid or recognized for helping someone else sell. So I don't do it."[2]

Salespeople may also be unwilling to share the rewards of making the sale. In other instances, the costs of drawing several people together to meet with the client can provoke skepticism about the impact of team selling on overall profitability.

---

[2]Cespedes et al., pp. 44–58.

The organizations that use team selling successfully have suggested these guidelines:

1. *Drive it from the top.* Communication of the organization's strategic goals and the salespeople's role in achieving them is critical. When team selling is one of the organization's tactics for achieving key goals, it has to be made a priority and endorsed at all levels of the organization—starting with the chief executive officer.

2. *Set clear criteria and goals.* Team selling should be used only for those customer situations that warrant it. When it is the chosen tactic, it should be guided by specific, measurable sales objectives and monitored for its effectiveness.

3. *Select an appropriate team structure.* Your teams' organizational structure influences their level of success. Different structures include *creative* teams, set up to optimize autonomy, and *tactical* teams, to execute a plan.[3] Whatever organizational structure is used, everyone on the team must clearly understand his or her role on the team— and should be held accountable for fulfilling that role.

4. *Compensate team members appropriately.* All the other measures to promote team selling will be in vain without an equitable compensation system. Common compensation solutions include establishing a bonus pool and sharing sales credit.

5. *Train team members for continuing success.* To ensure the success of team selling, top-performing organizations train team members in selling skills, interpersonal communication skills, and teamwork.

Xerox Corporation (United States), for example, considers training in interpersonal communication skills to be critical to the success of its team selling efforts. "We know that we have to work together effectively as teams," says a manager in the U.S. marketing group. "From sales, administration, and service—all of us are taught interpersonal communication skills so we can work together more effectively to meet the customer's needs."

Salespeople may initially be uncomfortable with team selling. However, they grow to accept and appreciate the change for one

---

[3]Cespedes et al., pp. 44–58.

A Salesperson's Checklist for Successful Team Selling

Before you meet with a customer. . .

- Decide on an objective for the sales call that defines what internal resources would be required. Include funding needed, computer time, type of personnel, etc.
- Describe the team selling process to the customer so he or she understands the value the team will add.
- Designate a team leader to manage the team. This doesn't have to be the salesperson. The individual with the most knowledge in the area of focus (based on the objective) could manage the work of the team.
- Identify each team member's role. Be sure to include individuals in the customer organization as well as your own.
- Define, specifically, how each individual's role will help the customer.
- Determine a process for sales calls.
- Practice (and practice again) the process for the sales call.

After the sales call. . .

- Conduct a debriefing session among the team members to share observations and ideas.
- Review commitments.
- Determine an action plan.
- Monitor the implementation and success of the action plan.

---

very simple reason: Team selling helps them sell better. "I was uncomfortable when I was introduced to team selling," said one salesperson. "But when I realized I just couldn't sell the product on my own, I learned to like it."

CONCLUSION

Customers today look for suppliers that can demonstrate much greater depth and breadth of knowledge about their businesses and the ability to deliver well-thought-out, customized, comprehensive solutions to their business challenges. Like symphony conductors, salespeople must be able to bring in the proper resources at the right time and coordinate the efforts of a number of people within both the customer and supplier organizations. They must accomplish this while ensuring that the customer's personal and organizational needs are met. Salespeople who excel as strategic orchestrators will create bonds with customers that are not easily broken.

BEST PRACTICES AND GUIDING PRINCIPLES

- Encourage your salespeople to take on the role of strategic orchestrator through the following practices:
  - Involve your company's decision makers in the customer's business.
  - Know the responsibilities of colleagues who are not salespeople.
  - Know the strengths and shortcomings of colleagues.
  - Coordinate the efforts of colleagues in all functions.
  - Maintain rapport with managers.
  - Seek assistance or guidance from others in the company.
  - Adopt a problem-solving approach to production, delivery, and service problems.
  - Anticipate the customer's concerns, and initiate the coordination necessary to satisfy the customer's current and future needs.
  - Weigh the costs and benefits associated with various value-adding activities, and assert the value of personal time and effort.
  - Initiate the coordination necessary to meet the customer's needs.
  - Facilitate communication between customers and the company's own research and development, sales management, or customer support personnel.
- Assess whether team selling should be a practice in your organization. Ask yourself the following:
  - Is team selling consistent with our organization's culture?
  - What do we hope to accomplish through team selling? How will it add value for our customers?

- What has our experience with team selling been? Under what conditions has it been helpful? What are some of the lessons learned?
- Do our competitors use team selling? What do we know about their success with it?
- When integrating team selling into your organization,
  - Communicate to all employees the reasons behind the shift to team selling, what you hope to accomplish with it, and how it will benefit your organization and customers.
  - Identify changes in your operations, processes, and organizational structure that would create an environment more conducive to team selling.
  - Identify and address factors that might inhibit the success of team selling. These include attitudes, structural barriers, communication channels, procedures, and policies.
  - Find ways to implement team selling systematically. Team selling should be a focus of training and coaching, as well as measurement and reward systems.
  - Ensure that:
    - Top management gives recognizable support to team selling. This includes recognition and rewards for executing it effectively and allocation of funding for training.
    - Everyone in the organization sees the value in team selling, is clear about the organization's team selling goal, and is committed to its success.

Chapter Six

Salesperson as Business Consultant

"The essential role of a salesperson is selling. But salespeople also need to be advisors: They must offer clients a full package of advice and service."

—Sales manager, Matra Communications (France)

- How do salespeople fulfill the role of business consultant?
- What practices and competencies are associated with this role?
- What information do salespeople need to be effective business consultants?
- How can you ensure that your salespeople have the right information?
- Why are electronic performance support systems important?

As we have seen from Learning International's research and discussion of the changing marketplace, customers expect more from salespeople than ever before. Beginning with the first interaction between a salesperson and customer, the customer looks for evidence of the salesperson's general business knowledge and ability to ask insightful, "big picture" questions about the customer's business needs and objectives. Figure 6–1 reviews the relationship among the three roles of a salesperson.

"Customers want to work with salespeople who are aware of the fast-moving business environment and are able to offer up-to-date advice," said a customer of BP Oil (The Netherlands). Most salespeople are aware of this customer expectation. Many talk

FIGURE 6–1
The Three Roles of the Consultative Salesperson

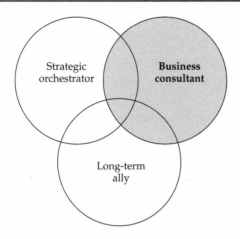

about the importance of "earning the right" to continue the sales discussions at each meeting. One respondent in the Learning International study said that his first task as a salesperson was to "get the customer to buy *me*." In other words, before salespeople can sell a product or service, they must first sell themselves—they must persuade the customers of their integrity, reliability, and ability to understand needs and recommend effective solutions.

Salespeople can demonstrate integrity and reliability by providing solid insights into the customer's business challenges and then offering straightforward guidance about the best way to meet those challenges. In so doing, the salesperson transcends the role of a supplier and becomes a valued **business consultant.**

Our research of top sales organizations around the world reveals three factors that have the most influence on a salesperson's ability to fulfill the role of business consultant. Those three factors are:

- Knowledge.
- Communication skills.
- Attitude.

In this chapter, we'll examine these factors and describe how they can help your salespeople step more easily into the role of

---

Business Consultant

A salesperson who fosters customer confidence and strengthens selling relationships by demonstrating:

• General business knowledge.
• A comprehensive understanding of the customer's business challenges.
• An ability to develop and help implement effective solutions and recommendations.

---

business consultant. We'll also look at how information management systems can enhance the effectiveness of any business consultant's approach.

KNOWLEDGE: BEYOND PRODUCTS AND SERVICES

"A salesperson must have the capacity and the intellect to absorb a tremendous amount of information and turn it into action that yields results quickly."

—Sales manager, Xerox Corporation (United States)

Because customers today are under pressure to accomplish more objectives using fewer resources, a growing number rely on salespeople to help them make effective business decisions. But there's a catch: Most customers don't have time to educate salespeople about their organization. Today they expect salespeople to come to the very first meeting prepared to discuss some of the deeper issues surrounding the customer's organization. Because customers have more supplier options available, they are impatient with salespeople who are unable to quickly demonstrate that they are knowledgeable business professionals and not simply persuasive "peddlers."

This is one of the greatest challenges salespeople face today. To add value for their customers, salespeople need to know a

---

Information for Competitive Advantage: Hewlett-Packard

Hewlett-Packard Company (United States) is an example of an organization that uses information to add value to its customer relationships. Since its customers deal with high-technology issues, they have extremely high technical literacy and sophistication. To ensure its salespeople can be business consultants to these customers, Hewlett-Packard provides its salespeople with tools to learn as much about their clients as about the technology they sell. Before they walk into a sales call, salespeople have conducted a thorough analysis of the customer. This analysis also involves becoming intimately familiar with other suppliers' products and how they might be integrated with Hewlett-Packard products. Armed with this knowledge, Hewlett-Packard salespeople are able to build a solution that involves complementary products from its many partners, and, when necessary, technological pieces from competitive companies. This is evidence of HP's commitment to help its customers find the best solutions.

---

significant amount about the customer's business at the start of every sales interaction. In other words, they have to know *more* when they walk in the door.

Top sales professionals become knowledgeable business consultants by:

1. *Demonstrating and refining their understanding of the customer's big-picture challenges and bottom-line realities.* "With both new and existing customers," said a salesperson with Northwestern Mutual Life Insurance Company (United States), "the salesperson must constantly be in tune with what the customer is thinking about." Effective business consultants at first set aside the question of potential for their own products and services. Instead, they use all resources and contacts available to gain a comprehensive understanding of:

   • The issues at all levels of the customer's organization, including strategic, departmental, and individual needs.

- The customer's perceptions of market trends, company direction, and potential product and service needs.

"Salespeople should have good knowledge of what is happening in the market and how their products can help customers keep up with the changes and evolutions," remarked a customer of BP Oil (The Netherlands). "Customers need up-to-date advice."

2. *Fostering the exchange of information and ideas.* Business consultants facilitate the free flow of information and ideas between their organization and their customers' organizations. As part of this effort, salespeople:

- Take the time needed to familiarize their customers with their own industry and companys.

- Share useful business information with customers, even when the information doesn't directly further their sales effort.

- Demonstrate the cost-cutting or revenue-producing benefits of their products and services.

3. *Continually strengthening their business knowledge.* Business consultants make a point of staying current with the business world at large, not just their own, or even their customers', particular field of specialization. They constantly look for the business trends that influence their customers' organizations, and any new opportunities these trends may offer toward helping their customers become more successful. To keep abreast of these trends, business consultants:

- Read newspapers, magazines, journals, trade publications, annual reports, and other sources of business information.

- Maintain memberships in appropriate professional organizations.

- Acknowledge gaps in their understanding or knowledge and then take steps to fill these gaps by soliciting information from appropriate sources.

- Locate or develop online or offline databases containing information on customers, their industries, and their customers.

COMMUNICATION SKILLS: BEYOND PERSUASION

"Communication skills are a must. I can't think of a good salesperson who doesn't know how to talk to people."
—Sales manager, Hewlett-Packard Company (United States)

In addition to being knowledgeable business professionals, effective business consultants are skilled communicators. No matter how brilliant and knowledgeable a salesperson may be, the information he or she brings to the sales call is useful to the customer only if the salesperson is able to express it clearly and in a way the customer understands and values.

This is not simply the ability to use compelling words when introducing or describing a product or service. Respondents in the Sales Leadership study said that the communication skills they value most in salespeople are the ability to ask effective questions, listen and demonstrate understanding, and express themselves clearly. Salespeople who fulfill the role of business consultant continually do the following:

1. *Sharpen their approach to identifying customers' needs.* Business consultants develop and continually fine-tune their ability to uncover customer needs. As a result, they are able to develop solutions that make sense for their customers' immediate and long-term objectives.

   A critical element in uncovering and analyzing customer needs is asking the right questions. In addition, salespeople need to be able to direct the discussion to focus on the customer's priorities and interests. Salespeople must actively listen to customers' comments to confirm their understanding of customers' needs and to determine customers' level of satisfaction with current products or services. In some cases, the salesperson helps customers identify needs that they may not realize they have. This is often the case when the product or service is complex or intangible. "In retail, people walk into a store and know what they need to buy," explained a sales manager with Northwestern Mutual Life Insurance Company (United States). "In our business, they may not even know that they have a need." Top salespeople never

stop asking questions;they never presume that they
understand the customer's business so well that they
don't need to constantly check their assumptions,
especially when developing solutions. Successful business
consultants:

- Confirm their understanding of each customer's mission,
  goals, strategies, markets, products and services, business
  functions, and competitors.
- Find out what customers must do to succeed in their jobs.

2. *Refine their communication skills.* Effective business consultants
   are always looking for ways to enhance communication skills
   that enable them to develop, explain, and implement
   solutions. They constantly:

- Speak at listeners' levels of knowledge and sophistication.
- Use stories and analogies effectively.
- Ask for feedback from customers on the clarity of their
  communication.

3. *Polish their presentation skills.* The ability to effectively
   present the recommended solution to the customer is
   critical. "Salespeople have to be good at presenting a
   package once they understand what the customer requires,"
   said a sales manager at Allen & Hanbury's (United
   Kingdom). For example, during most presentations, the
   salesperson must be able to:

- Describe the sales organization's capabilities.
- Introduce new or improved products and services.
- Make a proposal or offer a recommendation.
- Create a common understanding and/or facilitate
  an agreement among a group of buyers or decision
  makers.
- Gain the customer's agreement to buy or to take the next
  step in the sales process.

The clarity of the salesperson's presentation is the proof
for the customer of how well the salesperson understands
his or her needs. The logic and persuasiveness of
the recommendation demonstrate the salesperson's
ability to guide customers in achieving their desired
objective.

ATTITUDE: BEYOND POSITIVE THINKING

"Skills can be developed over time, but the right attitude has to be there from the beginning."
—Sales manager, Northwestern Mutual Life Insurance Company
(United States)

Have you ever met a salesperson whose knowledge and eloquence were dazzling . . . but whose attitude irritated you so much that it sabotaged any chance of a relationship between your two organizations?

The "right" attitude goes beyond the positive thinking that has characterized traditional how-to sales literature and speeches. According to the sales and customer organizations interviewed, the more effective business consultants are characterized in these ways:

- *"They are sensitive and perceptive."*

  —Sales manager, Xerox Corporation (United States)

- *"They are more like colleagues to us than salespeople."*

  —Customer, Boehme (Germany)

- *"They are motivated more by the intrinsic rewards than the extrinsic ones."*

  —Sales manager, Northwestern Mutual Life Insurance Company
  (United States)

- *"They are able to give up preconceived attitudes. Flexibility is their way of thinking."*

  —Sales manager, Bayerische Vereinsbank (Germany)

- *"They are always enthusiastic. They think around the situation and know how to turn a problem into an opportunity."*

  —Sales manager, Allen & Hanbury's (United Kingdom)

- *"They have high integrity. They are ethical and professional."*

  —Sales manager, Scott Paper Company (United States)

- *"They achieve goals that are based on their own clear vision."*

  —Area sales manager, Sony Corporation (Japan)

For all the discussion about business sophistication, the "right" attitude is still a critical element of successful selling.

THE INFORMATION REVOLUTION
COMES TO SELLING

"Selling is changing in two ways. First, it's becoming more consultative, which means bringing in a team with the right technical expertise, identifying customer needs, and selecting from a portfolio of solutions. Second, there's a revolution in information technologies that will have implications for prequalifying, internal support, and database marketing."

—Vice president, Scott Paper Company (United States)

At the beginning of the chapter, we discussed the critical role that knowledge plays in helping the salesperson fulfill the role of business consultant and how customers expect salespeople to be more knowledgeable than ever before.

The bad news is that the knowledge base salespeople need has expanded well beyond what any individual could possibly know. Salespeople need more information about products, services, customers, and competitors than ever before.

Often the need to gather and organize information lengthens the sales process. Also, the growing emphasis on team selling makes it critical to share information quickly and accurately among a wide variety of people who influence the account.

The good news is that technology has exploded the boundaries of today's knowledge frontiers: Salespeople have access to almost any conceivable piece of information or data.

Nearly every sales organization has invested in some sort of technology to automate certain steps in the sales process. In most cases, this technology helps salespeople use their pre-call time more efficiently, to access information about the client, for example. But many companies are looking for ways to use technology to improve salespeople's performance when they're *with* clients.

A new application of computer technologies, collectively known as electronic performance support systems (EPSS), is making this possible. Also referred to as integrated performance support systems (IPSS), an EPSS may be a shell program that accesses various information databases and links and organizes them with a minimum of effort on the part of the salesperson. An EPSS can often save the salesperson from having to interrupt the flow of a sales call to return to the office and gather information. It does this by allowing the salesperson to call up on his or her computer almost instantly the information necessary to make recommendations and assist the customer in making decisions *during* a sales call.

An example of an EPSS can be found at Intel Corporation (United States), which provides its 1,000 sales representatives with what it calls the "I Know" performance support system. Developed by Ariel Corporation (United States), the system is accessed on the rep's notebook computer during a sales call and lets the sales rep:

- Compare two Intel products side by side.
- Compare Intel products against a competitive product.
- Develop "if/then" sales scenarios with recommended answers.
- Create custom presentations.

The EPSS provides Intel salespeople with the means to keep up with information about new products and to get the information they need, when they need it. It also decreases the time they spend on fact-finding and improves customer responsiveness.

Information technology has also been used by American Airlines (United States) to add value on sales calls—and to create a competitive advantage. American Airlines has made a major investment in information technology to analyze the factors that influence its own profitability and that of the travel agencies that book its flights. The data, downloaded onto each sales rep's notebook PC every month, are used on sales calls with travel agents. The salesperson can show the agents the increase in American Airlines bookings and the effect on their agency's commissions and overall market share.

Until recently, that information was available only if travel agencies gathered it themselves. When another airline announced its intention to provide similar information, American Airlines offered theirs in an updated form and at more frequent intervals. By adding value through unique information, American Airlines's salespeople bring themselves into closer partnership with customers while simultaneously building American Airlines's share of its markets.

No matter which EPSS a company installs, however, it should be introduced in a logical fashion. Linsalata and Highland describe five common phases of a sales information system implementation, each one characterized by an increase in the amount of information shared with the customer:[1]

1. *Focus on providing the sales force with seamless communications and easy, convenient access to information.* During this stage, it is important to understand the company's strategy, as well as customers' needs, and to focus on identifying the information requirements of the customer and the sales process. Avoid the traditional systems engineering focus of automating existing manual procedures.

2. *Provide decision-support tools to leverage the newly available information.* An example would be a rules-based system that makes sales recommendations.

3. *Optimize the use of these technologies by re-engineering the sales force to assume greater decision-making authority* and manage a broader range of products and customers. This involves releasing increasing amounts of information, responsibility, and authority from corporate headquarters to the sales organization.

4. *Integrate the customer's information systems to transfer some time-consuming tasks to the customer.* Some examples might be preliminary price quotes, product availability, order entry, and new product introductions. With more time available, the sales rep can work with the customer on value-added projects and proposals.

5. *Review and refine the process to improve the customer-supplier relationship.* During this stage, it may be necessary to enhance the sales information system to support new customer requirements.

In addition, EPSSs have advantages outside the sales arena. For example, their ability to merge databases gives suppliers greater ability to capture and analyze information on how their customers buy products. This information can then be shared with

---

[1]Ralph Linsalata and Richard Highland, "Re-engineering the Selling Process," white paper published by Eavoiy Systems Corporation (Waltham, MA).

TABLE 6–1
Potential Impact of Electronic Performance
Support Systems on a Sales Cycle

Factor	Without EPSS	With EPSS
Level of product knowledge the salesperson needs	Specific knowledge of all key products the company and competitors offer.	General knowledge of relevant company and competitive products, since the EPSS provides detailed information.
Where information exists	Primarily in databases and catalogues.	In connected databases.
How information can be accessed and organized	Salesperson or assistant locates and organizes information. This requires considerable backstage work.	Salesperson or customer uses EPSS to access and organize information instantly. Minimal backstage work is required.
Length of sales cycle	Longer, since sales calls are often terminated when further information is needed.	Shorter, since much more information is available during sales calls.

the customer to permit more informed purchasing decisions. It can also be shared with the sales organization to make informed decisions about the marketplace.

In short, EPSS can dramatically increase the flexibility and responsiveness of a salesperson on a call, whereas traditional sales force technologies focus primarily on reducing costs by automating mechanical, repetitive processes (see comparison in Table 6–1).

CONCLUSION

The credibility of the salesperson is a critical factor in developing relationships with customers. Today, credibility is built by demonstrating comprehensive knowledge, outstanding communication skills, and the proper attitude. In this way, salespeople can fulfill the new role of business consultant.

BEST PRACTICES AND GUIDING PRINCIPLES

- From the start, salespeople have to build credibility by demonstrating general business knowledge and asking insightful questions—for instance, questions that get customers to think about issues and opportunities of which they may not have been aware. Knowledge can be demonstrated by discussing the customer's big-picture challenges and bottom line realities, as well as what the customer has to do to personally succeed.

- Encourage your salespeople to take on the role of business consultant through the following practices:

  - Use contacts to acquire information about a customer's business.

  - Seek customers' and colleagues' perceptions of market trends, company direction, and potential product/service needs.

  - Find out what customers must do to succeed in their jobs.

  - Identify issues and needs at all levels (e.g., overriding business issues, organizational issues and priorities, functional and individual issues or needs).

  - Find or develop online or offline databases containing information on customers, industries, and the customers' own customers.

  - Confirm understanding of each customer's mission, goals, strategies, markets, products/services, business functions, and competitors.

  - Familiarize customers with your industry or company.

  - Read newspapers, magazines, business journals, trade publications, and annual reports; attend conferences to increase knowledge of business and industries.

  - Demonstrate the cost-cutting or revenue-producing benefits of products/services.

  - Share useful business information with customers, even when it doesn't directly further the sales effort.

  - Speak at listeners' levels of knowledge and sophistication.

  - Use stories and analogies effectively.

  - Seek feedback from customers on the clarity of communications.

- Acknowledge gaps in understanding or knowledge.
- Develop solutions in which the customer, supplier organization, and salespeople all "win."
- Never stop exploring ways to put relevant, up-to-date information into the salesperson's hands on a "just-in-time" basis. This will allow salespeople to focus more on the problem and the customer rather than on technical details of products, services, and solutions.

Chapter Seven

Salesperson as Long-Term Ally

"Sales activities continue long after you have sold the product. The objective is not only to get the sale, but to have customers use the product after buying it. That's why post-sale and follow-up are true sales activities. They are the key to profits and repeat orders."

—Sales representative, Fuji Xerox Company (Japan)

- What do customers value in long-term relationships?
- How are alliances built?
- What is meant by the relationship gap?
- How can the relationship gap be closed?

Chapter Four discussed consultative selling as a critical strategy for many of the world's leading sales organizations. It enables them to develop the rapport, trust, and respect needed to strengthen customer relationships and gain competitive advantage. Chapters Five and Six examined the roles that strategic orchestrators and business consultants play in effective selling. This chapter examines the third role of consultative selling: long-term ally. Figure 7–1 again demonstrates the three roles of the salesperson.

CUSTOMER'S PERSPECTIVE ON LONG-TERM ALLIANCES

"The salesperson helps me look good in my organization and offers solutions where we both profit."

—Customer, Boehme (Germany)

FIGURE 7–1
Three Roles of the Consultative Salesperson

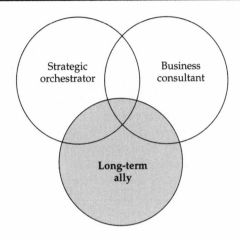

Sometimes, less is more. A study of Fortune 1000 companies, conducted by the National Association of Purchasing Management,[1] reveals the 10 most important trends that will influence purchasing decisions in the future. As Table 7–1 shows, purchasing managers ranked *reducing* the number of suppliers they work with as the single most important change in the way they work with suppliers. In addition, those surveyed agree that this change will also be the most important trend in the future, extending into the twenty-first century.

There are many reasons why customers want to work with fewer suppliers:

- Because the demands of their own customers change rapidly, buyers do not have the time to constantly experiment with or "break in" a new supplier. They must limit the number of supplier organizations with which they work. The organizations they choose to work with must be able to provide reliable, flexible support before, during, and after the sale.

---

[1]As described in *Personal Selling Power* magazine, September 1993. Barry Retchfeld, *Personal Selling Power*, 13, no. 6, pp. 26-33.

TABLE 7–1
Purchasing Trends Ranked in Order of Importance

Current	Future	Trend
1	1	Fewer sources of supply will be used
3	2	Customer satisfaction will count more for purchases
2	3	Purchasers will manage supplier relations
4	4	Purchasers will aim for shorter cycle times
6	5	Supply chain management will receive greater emphasis
7	6	Engineers and buyers will work together as a team
8	7	Purchasers will buy more from foreign producers
10	8	Ordering will be more decentralized
9	9	Teams will choose suppliers
5	10	Single sourcing will increase

- In addition, the decisions customers make today are much more complex and more likely to have a direct impact on the company's strategic direction than ever before.[2]

- As a result, customers expect to work with salespeople and supplier organizations who understand their strategies and can develop solutions to a wide range of immediate- and long-term needs. They expect to work with salespeople who can fulfill the roles of strategic orchestrator, business consultant, and long-term ally throughout the business relationship.

The implication for sales organizations is clear. Any sales organization that hopes to meet these customer expectations must have salespeople who are able to position themselves and the company as a **long-term ally.**

Top-performing sales organizations around the world say that developing long-term relationships with customers will be absolutely critical to the success of their business.

---

[2]For more information, see Chapter Two.

*Associated Spring: Building Long-Term Relationships
with Suppliers[3]*

Theresa Metty, director of materials for Associated Spring, part of the Barnes Group in Bristol, Connecticut, (United States) has headed up the development of a comprehensive supplier relations program that has cut the number of suppliers by more than half.

"We are interested in building much longer term relationships now than in past years," Metty says. "We used to have suppliers who were in and out and then back again. Now, once in, they stay in as long as they can perform. Instead of having several suppliers for a given commodity, we now have perhaps two. That's as low as we can go without endangering continuity of supply."

The advantage, says Metty, is that her company knows it can count on those two suppliers, and they know they can count on Associated Spring. If a supplier has problems, Associated Spring will work with the supplier intensively rather than shutting it off as it used to.

BUILDING ALLIANCES

"Salespeople must constantly keep track of each customer's situation, how it has changed, and what the customer wants to do about it. They can't assume the customer's situation is stable or that their needs stay the same."

—Salesperson, Northwestern Mutual Life Insurance Company
(United States)

What can salespeople do to put themselves and their organizations on the road to long-term alliances with their customers? Research identified 20 practices that characterize successful long-term allies, based upon surveys completed by 650 salespeople and 155 sales managers in 13 companies throughout North America. The best salespeople actively display a

---

[3]James S. Howard, "Suppliers and Customers Put Down the Gloves," *D & B Reports* 41, no. 3 (May/June 1992), pp. 26–28.

Long-Term Ally

A salesperson who demonstrates commitment—and is able to contribute—to the customer's short- and long-term success throughout the entire Customer Relationship Process.

---

long-term perspective of the relationship and a commitment to their customers' future. They do this by continually looking for ways to:

- Build interpersonal trust.
- Create and sustain a positive image of the sales organization.
- Inspire respect for their company.
- Demonstrate concern for their customers' long-term, as well as immediate, interests.
- Identify ways to strengthen the quality of their business relationships.
- Help the customer meet needs within his or her organization.
- Resolve issues openly and honestly.
- Deliver on promises.

Another critical activity for the salesperson is to ensure that the relationship between the two organizations is mutually beneficial. At the heart of the concept of being long-term allies is an expectation that the agreements will be good business for both organizations.

Sales managers across all industries have strong opinions about the need to develop a balance, or a sense of fairness and equity, in the partnership between the buyer and seller organizations. This is a marked difference in attitude since Learning International's customer service research was conducted several years ago. At that time, supplier organizations said that they were "adding value" by offering the customer more and more at less and less cost. Today, organizations are more sophisticated about the need to maintain profitability *and* achieve customer satisfaction and the importance of making trade-offs to achieve both goals in the long run.

TABLE 7–2
Long-Term Allies and Mutually Beneficial Agreements

Supplier Organization Must Be Willing to . . .	Buyer Organization Must Be Willing to . . .
Solicit feedback from customers regarding overall satisfaction with the products/services delivered	Keep suppliers "in the loop" regarding the company's strategic direction and needs
Maintain regular contact with current and prospective customers	Value the record of service provided by supplier organization above lower-cost competitors
Alert customers to new developments in own organization	Grant access and information about their customers to the supplier organization
Review the business relationship underlying each account regularly	

In a British research study, Eugene Fram and Martin Presberg interviewed 133 sales managers to examine supplier experiences with purchasing partners. Many lamented the inordinate burden suppliers must bear in maintaining mutually profitable relationships. Over time, said the managers, customers typically ask for the most costly services, "cherry pick" low-margin items to the detriment of the supplier, or withhold information on needs and goals. In most cases, it's up to the supplier to resolve these strains or find solutions both parties can live with.[4]

What does a successful alliance entail? While every alliance is different, the ones we studied have several characteristics in common. They are summarized in Table 7–2.

One organization that is committed to developing long-term relationships is Xerox Corporation (United States). Acting as long-term allies to their customers, Xerox sales professionals cultivate relationships by building trust, researching options, and offering recommendations designed to solve the customer's strategic business problems.

Xerox believes that the partnership role will be increasingly significant in helping companies survive global competition during

---

[4]Reported in the *Journal of Business and Industrial Marketing* 8, no. 4 (1993).

the next decade. This sales approach is delivering more profits to Xerox than the "make a sale at any cost" approach of the past.

In the European food industry, leading suppliers such as Unilever and Procter & Gamble are developing partnerships with their key customers. These partnerships go well beyond traditional buyer/seller relationships. They involve all aspects of the organization, including the links between account managers and category managers, between the logistics operations of both sides, between accounts outgoing and receiving. Electronic data interchange (EDI) is one element of how these organizations achieve major savings through closer relationships.

To develop a successful alliance, salespeople must focus on the customers' customers. Ultimately, the customers' success is based on their ability to meet and exceed their own customers' expectations. A salesperson's success will largely depend on how well he or she helps them do that. "What's unique about Scott," said one distributor of Scott Paper Company (United States), "is that they don't think of the distributor as the ultimate customer. We work in partnership with them to reach the end user. They always keep in mind that the end user is the ultimate customer. This is different from most of their competitors who think of the distributor as the ultimate customer. Scott really understands the idea of partnership and they really believe it."

CLOSING THE RELATIONSHIP GAP

"In a competitive society, the customer's demands are, in a sense, absolute. We commit ourselves to meeting the customer's expectations and building a trustworthy relationship."

—Senior general manager of component marketing group, Sony Corporation (Japan)

The ability of a salesperson to fulfill the role of long-term ally is a pivotal factor in determining whether a sales interaction is just a *transaction* or the beginning of a relationship. The focus on long-term relationships is a dramatic change from the way sales organizations, and salespeople, have traditionally defined their roles. As shown in Figure 7–2, many salespeople have considered their roles fulfilled when the sale is made. However, there

Partners and Long-Term Allies

When it comes to describing the desired, long-term state of affairs between customers and sales organizations, many different terms are used interchangeably. The most common ones used today are "partnership" and "relationship."

The term *partnership* often describes a comprehensive and strategic relationship between two organizations—one in which the two companies have made a formal commitment to work together to achieve a shared objective. In some cases, the companies may even agree to change their business processes to accommodate each other.

The ability of a salesperson to fulfill the role of long-term ally is critical to the success of partnerships and long-term business relationships.

FIGURE 7–2
Managing the Relationship Gap

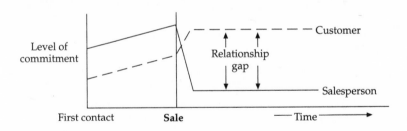

Source: Mark Jenkins, Cranfield School of Management, 1994.

is a tremendous opportunity to develop a long-term relationship by fulfilling the role of the long-term ally long *after* the sale.

Figure 7–2 shows a typical relationship between a buyer and seller over time. Initially, the customer's level of commitment to the process is low, and the supplier's level of commitment is high. After the sale, the salesperson's interest in dealing with the customer's concerns often drops substantially. Conversely, after the sale, the customer's interest in the success of the implementation increases rapidly. The vast difference between their post-sale levels of concern has been referred to as the *relationship gap.*

Salespeople who fulfill the role of long-term ally work to eliminate the relationship gap by ensuring that the customer is receiving the level of support and service that meets his or her expectation now *and* throughout the duration of the Customer Relationship Process.

CONCLUSION

The limited resources that all companies face in today's business environment are driving the need to build stronger bonds between suppliers and customers and to develop long-term relationships.

Salespeople who are able to position themselves as long-term allies earn the right to be one of the customer's long-term suppliers. In so doing, they help their companies stand out in the marketplace and contribute to their growth and prosperity.

BEST PRACTICES AND GUIDING PRINCIPLES

- Encourage your salespeople to take on the role of long-term ally through the following practices:
  - Identify opportunities to make personal commitments and keep the commitments they make.
  - Seize the opportunities to convey pride and confidence in the products/services and respect for the way the company operates.
  - Fully educate prospective users about product features, benefits, and applications.
  - Educate customers about a competitor's products/services (when appropriate).
  - Respond thoroughly and honestly to customer concerns.
  - Position the capabilities and shortcomings of your products and organization realistically, and highlight the positives of your own products and organization instead of the negatives of your competitors' products or organizations.

- Make recommendations on the basis of customers' long-term needs, not on what the salesperson needs to sell.
- Turn down business not in the customers' long-term interests.
- "Go to bat" for customers within your company.
- Negotiate contracts in which customers *and* one's own company win in the long run.
- Regularly assert availability and desire to be of service.
- Identify ways to make customers look good in the eyes of their own colleagues and superiors.
- Help customers carry out fact-finding or "selling" strategies within their own company.
- Elicit information from customers that helps them define and strengthen the direction of future business.
- Maintain contact with customers even when there's no prospect of an immediate sale.
- Foster mutual respect by asking for—as well as providing—assistance, information, and honesty.
- Identify information and services that salespeople could provide that would be valuable to customers.
- "Go the extra mile" whenever necessary—for instance, help customers carry out fact-finding missions.

P A R T

III

CRITICAL SUCCESS
FACTORS

"The salesperson is the ambassador of the company."

Chapter Eight

Strategic Sales Training

"Properly training salespeople to make sure they can effectively compete is one of the biggest challenges facing companies today."

—Sales manager, Xerox Corporation (United States)

- What is strategic sales training?
- How can training help to communicate a strategic vision?
- Is there a model for strategic training?
- What are the characteristics of strategic training?
- What are some trends in training?

The concepts and ideas that we've discussed in this book—from customer loyalty to consultative selling to the salesperson as strategic orchestrator, business consultant, and long-term ally—are powerful strategies that the world's top-performing sales organizations are using to achieve competitive differentiation. These are strategies that are brought to life and executed consistently by salespeople who understand the implications for their daily sales practices. One of the most powerful methods to achieve this is **strategic sales training.**

ONE VISION, CLEARLY COMMUNICATED

"Our sales training is directed at the critical strategic areas of our business."

—Vice president, Bayerische Vereinsbank (Germany)

Sales executives and training managers at top-performing organizations agree that the best sales training decisions are linked to an

---

Sales Training

The process of providing a salesperson or sales team member with the skills, knowledge, and attitudes necessary to increase that person's productivity.

Strategic Sales Training

The use of sales training to achieve a sales strategy in a systematic way.

---

organization's key business objectives. To establish this link at your company, each person in your sales and sales training organizations should be able to answer the following question:

How should our salespeople sell differently to meet the changing market conditions of today and tomorrow?

Some organizations have been able to answer this in a way that is easily understood at all levels. In doing so, these companies create a common language in which all employees discuss the organization's sales strategy and develop activities that support that strategy. Creating this kind of unity requires tremendous focus, discipline, and leadership.

Hewlett-Packard (United States) is one company that has achieved this common understanding and commitment. Every person we interviewed at Hewlett-Packard expressed a clear understanding of the company's competitive issues, goals, and their sales organization's key strategies. Most strikingly, three levels of sales managers, several sales representatives, and the vice president of sales all described the sales strategy using similar words and phrases. Moreover, each had a clear understanding of the tasks they needed to complete to help achieve the company's objectives.

Another example of this kind of organization-wide understanding is Northwestern Mutual Life Insurance Company (United States), where the company mission statement—written by its founders in 1888—is still relevant today:

The ambition of The Northwestern has been less to be large than to be safe; its aim is to rank first in benefits to policyowners rather than first in size. Valuing quality above quantity, it has preferred to secure its business under certain salutary restrictions and limitations rather than to write a much larger business at the possible sacrifice of those valuable points which have made The Northwestern pre-eminently the policyowner's company.

Northwestern Mutual's mission statement guides the daily activities of all its divisions and departments, serving as a philosophical and ethical cornerstone and a clear statement about their values.

A key strength at these and other top sales organizations is that sales training directors are as familiar with their company's business strategies as sales executives and the line operation. The sales training directors have an understanding of how their company's markets are changing, the sales strategies being used to adapt to those changes, and the roles that salespeople have to fulfill to execute the sales strategies. They are able to discuss the competencies as well as the design and implementation issues of a training solution.

As Table 8–1 reveals, sales executives, sales operations managers, and sales training managers must share a vision of the markets, strategies, and appropriate training responses if the company is to successfully meet its objectives.

Where there is no shared vision, confusion and mixed signals reign. Sales executives may mistakenly believe that they are providing enough information to guide decisions about training. Some sales training managers may sense that they are missing information but aren't sure how to describe what they're missing.

In fact, every organization intends its sales training to support its sales strategies. The greatest risk for any organization is to *assume* that this is happening. One training manager we met talked at length about his company's training programs, schedules, and the number of hours of training each salesperson receives. But he was much less specific, and clearly uncomfortable, when asked how sales training was able to help his company differentiate itself from competition or to bring a specific strategy to life.

TABLE 8–1
Ideal Profile of Shared Information

Area	Sales Executives	Sales Operations	Sales Training Group
How markets are changing	✓	✓	✓
How sales strategies are changing	✓	✓	✓
The new roles of the salesperson	✓	✓	✓
How salespeople must sell differently	✓	✓	✓
New skills, knowledge, and attitudes	—	✓	✓
Designing, implementing, assessing, and improving training	—	—	✓

DYNAMIC MARKETS, CHANGING NEEDS: MODEL FOR STRATEGIC SALES TRAINING

"We use sales training to respond to the increasing challenge of our markets."

—Vice President, Scott Paper Company (United States)

Today's volatile markets and intense competition often require dramatic and rapid changes in an organization's sales strategy, changing the essential nature of the sales calls that the organization's salespeople conduct with customers.

Many organizations today are focusing on time-based strategies such as reducing cycle times to increase their responsiveness to market opportunities. As Stalk and Hout proposed in *Competing Against Time*, the results of compressing time are impressive. As time is compressed, the following changes occur:

- Productivity increases.
- Prices can be increased.
- Risks are reduced.
- Share is increased.[1]

---

[1]George, Stalk, Jr., and Thomas M. Hout, *Competing Against Time* (New York: The Free Press, 1990).

Strategic sales training plays a role in supporting time-based competition by ensuring that strategies are communicated and executed quickly and consistently.

The great irony of most sales training today is that it is training salespeople for *yesterday's* sales strategies and market conditions. By the time the training needs have been clearly identified, the programs designed and implemented, and sales managers trained in how to coach the programs, several months or even years may have passed—by which time the market may have changed substantially again.

Just as you update your strategy when the market changes, you should update your sales training, too.

To make sure that sales training is relevant and focuses on today's strategies and practices, sales training directors in the leading sales organizations are taking the initiative to ensure that they have a current comprehensive understanding of today's sales strategies. Based on our discussions with them, and on our own experience developing and implementing sales training, we have developed a model for strategic sales training (see Table 8–2). Executing each of these steps well will help ensure that your sales training directly supports your sales strategy. Each of these activities is crucial to achieving effective strategic sales training. If any of these steps is skipped or executed poorly, the effectiveness will be diminished.

The strategic sales training model illustrates how to use training as a critical tool that brings a sales strategy to life. Training can be used to communicate a strategy and define what the salespeople need to do to sell successfully.

TABLE 8–2
A Model for Strategic Sales Training

Activities	Key Questions
1. Describe company strategy.	What changes are occurring in the market regarding customers, technology, and competition?
	What is our strategy to differentiate us from competition?
2. Describe sales strategy.	How will the sales organization help differentiate the company?
	How can the sales organization add value beyond that already provided by products and services?
3. Build commitment to the strategies.	Does everyone in the sales organization have a common understanding of the company strategy and the sales strategy?
	Does everyone have a high level of commitment?
	Is there an understanding of how the organization, and every individual, will benefit from supporting the strategy?
4. Identify new roles.	What new roles will your salespeople fulfill to execute the sales strategy?
	Are the roles of strategic orchestrator, business consultant, and long-term ally important?
5. Determine new ways of selling.	How will salespeople have to sell differently to carry out the new roles?
	What competencies (knowledge, skills, and attitudes) do salespeople need to sell differently?
	Will activities in the Customer Relationship Process require new competencies?
6. Identify training needs.	What are competency strengths and weaknesses?
	What competencies should the training target for improvement?
7. Describe ideal training design.	What content and methodology should be included?
8. Implement training.	How can the quality of implementation be ensured?
	How can learning be reinforced?
	What coaching and follow-up activities are intended?
9. Assess training.	Is new learning being used on the job? What is the impact?
10. Improve training.	What needs to be improved, and how can it be done?

Union Pacific Railroad Gets Back on Track with Training[2]

Deregulation has caused significant upheaval in many industries, including the U.S. transportation industry. For Union Pacific Railroad, it became clear in 1987 that drastic action was needed if they were to win back more customers, gain market share, and achieve what must have appeared to many an impossible goal of providing world-class transportation service.

They implemented an eight-pronged total quality strategy to better meet the needs of their customers. "Training was perhaps the most important aspect of our overall improvement strategy," said the director of marketing and sales training. "We wanted to start with the basics, then add new courses to build on skills as they were acquired. And we decided to make the training mandatory—starting at the top. The importance of the training had to be demonstrated through leadership.

"We also decided that the training would be focused primarily on sales and marketing," he added. "If we were to meet customer requirements, we had to find out what those requirements were. The people in the best position to do that, the people closest to the customer, were our sales and marketing people."

Union Pacific started with a series of core programs that focused on the skills needed to uncover customer needs and establish rapport with customers. Training provided salespeople with the ability to explain the benefits of Union Pacific's total quality to its customers.

Top management also used these sessions to explain Union Pacific's overall strategies and to define the link between training and the positive contribution that the new skills could make to participants' careers and the company's prosperity.

To keep the positive momentum going, Union Pacific reinforced the training with additional skills and with coaching. Training sales managers to be coaches was only one element of a comprehensive strategy, but it played a key role in the company's dramatic turnaround. "You can't overestimate the importance of good, ongoing coaching," the director said. "It's critical that you have the right people in those jobs, with the mindset and the skills needed to help your salespeople continually improve."

In the ensuing years, Union Pacific Railroad leapt out of the doldrums, with net income growing from $440 million in 1987 to $667 million in 1992.

---

[2]James P. King, "Union Pacific Gets Back on Track with Training," *Training and Development* (August 1993), pp. 30–37.

SYSTEMATIC TRAINING PLAN

"The purpose of training is to provide practice. Otherwise, we have to practice on customers."

—Vice president, American Airlines (United States)

For generations, many sales organizations have been staunch advocates of on-the-job training for salespeople. They emphasized the fact that the most effective way for salespeople to improve was through experience, and that their skills would be sharpened over time as they gained more experience in working with actual customers.

But in today's market, customers simply cannot afford to be tutors for salespeople. They have too many pressures of their own, and they can't afford the time needed to "break in" a new salesperson for a supplier organization. Nor can they tolerate the ripple effect that a new salesperson's mistakes could have.

Most sales organizations can't afford this risk, either. The sink-or-swim approach of on-the-job training puts unnecessary strain on a customer relationship—if it doesn't break it entirely. Leading sales organizations have found that a better alternative to practicing in front of customers is to have their salespeople practice in structured settings with other salespeople: in a word, training.

"Training gives salespeople confidence, product knowledge, and a structure to implement it in front of a customer," noted a field sales manager from Allen & Hanbury's (United Kingdom). "People have to get better to survive in more difficult market situations," added a vice president from Océ (France). "One of the ways that they can improve is through training."

The sales organizations that are the most satisfied with their training share the following characteristics:

1. *Sales training is linked to a sales strategy.* Communications about the training make a clear link between the strategy and the training. Any case studies and examples used in the training are relevant to the strategy, as are the skills, knowledge, and attitudes taught in the training.
2. *Training is designed, planned, and implemented to achieve specific objectives.* The expectations and goals for the training are clearly stated.

3. *Training is implemented as a continuous process.* Training is provided at regular intervals throughout each salesperson's career.

4. *Training is supported with follow-up and coaching.* Reinforcement and applications workshops help ensure that new skills learned during the training are actually practiced on the job. Salespeople receive feedback on their performance during regular sales coaching calls.

5. *Sales policies and procedures are consistent with the objectives of the training.* Sales compensation, for example, does not encourage or tempt salespeople to work with their accounts in ways that are different from the practices they learned in training.

TRENDS IN TRAINING

"The ultimate training is 'just-in-time' and 'just-for-me.'"

—Director of PHH University, PHH Corporation (United States)

Sales training plays an important role within each of the sales organizations that participated in the sales leadership research. That role is changing everyday as business pressures and available opportunities change. The following are some important trends in training.

Different segments and channels will require different training.

"The important thing about training is what can I do with it tomorrow and the day after?"

—Training manager, Océ (The Netherlands)

- The increased costs of face-to-face selling will cause organizations to segment and target their customers more specifically in both business and consumer sales. Telemarketing and alternative distribution channels will be used more often. Training will support the skills and abilities required for success in each segment and channel.

Sales training will address a more complex sales environment.

"The salesperson has to acquire expert knowledge, and has to translate that knowledge into a language customers are able to understand,"

—Training manager, Bayerische Vereinsbank (Germany)

Allen & Hanbury's: Selling Against Competition

Over the past decade, the pharmaceutical industry in the United Kingdom has become far more competitive, and the battle for market share has become more intense. In addition, the industry has become a massive business.

Tighter government controls and other policy changes in the National Health Service have made hospitals and individual clinic practices more price sensitive and more demanding in their expectations of the pharmaceutical companies that sell to them. These customers want their time to be used effectively; they expect sales reps to be knowledgeable, to solve problems, and to be flexible in making decisions and responding to their needs. As a result, pharmaceutical companies have to be sharper about finding competitive advantages. In this business environment, the role of training is essential.

"Training is very focused on the job salespeople are expected to do," says Allen & Hanbury's training manager. The firm's salespeople go through a 12-week training program. The first five weeks consist of training in the field and in the head office. Selling skills training helps them obtain product knowledge and, using role plays, learn to focus more on the customer's needs. The next six weeks are spent in the field calling on customers, supported by a field trainer. The final week is spent in the office, training to refresh their knowledge and skills.

When all the training is complete, targets for competence levels are set for each rep at three- and six-month intervals. Individual performance is tracked through their trainers, and additional training and product refreshers are given to address shortfalls. To ensure that the new skills are practiced and applied, each representative creates a learning contract that identifies his or her goals and an action plan to achieve them.

Coaching plays a vital role in guiding the salespeople. Regional managers assess the representatives' performance in all areas through field observation—approximately 20 days spent with each rep in the field, per year. They observe the use of skills and knowledge in action and provide feedback. The field trainers do the same, typically spending from 8 to 16 days per year with each rep. In addition, the reps attend local training seminars, run by field trainers, and use videos to coach on selling skills. "It is absolutely essential to make those skills second nature," says the vice president for sales.   *(continued)*

Allen & Hanbury's: Selling Against Competition (concluded)

In the future, salespeople will receive more general business training. "We want our representatives to understand why the customers behave the way they do, as businesspeople. We also want to give them the ability and confidence to have more autonomy, so they can make more business decisions locally," says the training manager.

- Face-to-face communication skills will remain a primary focus in sales training. Consultative selling, for example, requires skillful listening and questioning.
- Self-led sales teams and team selling will continue to increase in importance and so will team skills: orchestration of individuals, team dynamics, and leadership. Training in teams will prepare members for their individual sales roles.
- The importance of product knowledge training will increase.
- Sales training will emphasize the wider range of knowledge required for consultative selling. General business knowledge and business management skills will increase in importance as salespeople run their territories in a more entrepreneurial manner.

Sales training will be more practical.

"As a sales organization, we need to know how a customer makes decisions and how we provide value in that context. As a training organization, we need to prepare our sales and service organizations to deliver that."

—Vice president, Xerox Corporation (United States)

- Training will reflect the changes in the customers' needs and expectations and in the organization's sales strategy. It will also emphasize selling to more senior management. "They must be able to discuss the relationship of our products to business issues with senior executives," asserted a vice president, Hewlett-Packard (United States).

Sales training will be evaluated more methodically.

"Companies must systematically identify training needs, build content into training programs based on job information, and evaluate training in terms

of the objectives for which it was designed. Only then will the field of training and development cease to be an art form that is dependent on the persuasiveness of the advocates, and instead be a science that is repeatable by others."[3]

- Virtually every training professional recognizes that systematic evaluation of training is a crucial need.
- The measurement of training will be used to focus on process improvement, not just on justifying the training—on *improving*, not just *proving*.[4]

Sales training will be more specific to the needs of the individual.

"The key thing is to ensure that the salespeople want to do something about their particular development area, so they are keen to progress. If the training is dovetailed to suit those requirements, you will succeed."

—Sales manager, Allen & Hanbury's (United Kingdom)

- Identification of an individual's strengths and weaknesses is a key to the success of training.

There will be more just-in-time training.

"We are incorporating the just-in-time concept—for example, data on customer satisfaction—into our training department to find ways to get information to salespeople at the moment they need it."

—Training manager, Northwestern Mutual Life Insurance Company (United States)

---

[3]K. N. Wexley and G. P. Latham, *Developing and Training Human Resources in Organizations* (New York: HarperCollins, 1991), p. 91.

[4]D. L. Kirkpatrick, "Techniques for Evaluating Training Programs," *Training Director's Journal* (November 1959). One classic model for evaluating training is Kirkpatrick's four levels of validation:

Level I validation answers the question, "How did participants feel about the training?" Interviews or questionnaires can be used to answer this question. The results reveal what may be done to improve seminar procedures or content to make the training more valuable to participants.

Level II validation answers the question, "Were learning objectives met?" Tests or work simulations can help answer this question.

Level III validation answers the "transfer of training" question; in other words, "Are salespeople demonstrating appropriate use of competencies on the job?" Behavioral observations, interviews, or customer satisfaction results can shed some light on this.

Level IV validation answers the question, "Are the objectives of training being met?" Revenues or customer satisfaction results again may answer this question.

- Just-in-time training means providing training when it is needed. It can also mean using information immediately to make adjustments in training programs.

Sales training will be a systematic process.

"If you want to accomplish a culture change, it is critical to train the sales managers first. That way, the managers can be teachers and leaders. Otherwise, they are followers, and are forced to be reactive."

—Sales manager, Xerox Corporation (United States)

- Instead of a series of discrete training events, sales training will be a more continuous learning process that addresses the needs of salespeople as they progress along a career path. It will be more systematic in its implementation, including more organized reinforcement, follow-up, and coaching to ensure that what is learned in training is actually incorporated into each salesperson's daily activities.
- Sales training will include managers more frequently, and at an earlier stage, to ensure that they know what their salespeople are learning. Coaching training for sales managers and others will prepare them to be teachers and leaders who provide better on-the-job feedback to salespeople. In some companies, such as Océ (France), managers are actually involved in the delivery of sales training. It refreshes their basic skills and works to improve the camaraderie within a sales team.

Sales training will be delivered in innovative ways.

"A one-way, lecture-type training program is not effective. Training participation is important."

—Training manager, Sony Corporation (Japan)

- As teleconferencing technology improves and expands, companies will find it easier to provide "distance learning." This will expand the concept of the virtual classroom and provide a less expensive alternative to traditional seminar-based programs that may involve substantial travel cost. Interactive computer software, delivered via CD-ROM and CDI (interactive CD), is another technology alternative.

Sales training will include nontraditional populations.

"Training will be done by the same company for the buyer and for the salesperson."

—Training manager, Ordo (France)

- Buyers and sellers will participate in training together, as partners.

Sales training will be used to reinforce global strategies.

"We must train to handle future challenges, not train to handle what has already happened."

—Salesperson, Rank Xerox (Sweden)

- As companies become global in scope, training will be used to create a sales culture within a worldwide organization that is based on a common set of values and skills, yet responsive to the demands of local markets.

CONCLUSION

"The acquisition of knowledge is a journey, not a destination."

—Vice president, Northwestern Mutual Life Insurance Company (United States)

With the profound changes taking place in today's market every organization has to be more nimble than ever. Each sales director must constantly re-evaluate the sales strategy in relation to the changes taking place. But it's not enough to simply adjust the strategy; it is more important than ever that the entire organization be prepared to execute the strategy effectively and reliably.

It is critical that those responsible for designing and implementing training have the information and support they need to make those changes faster and more effectively.

Everyone in the sales organization should be focused on ensuring that there is a tight connection between sales training and sales strategy—that the sales training your organization provides is truly strategic sales training.

BEST PRACTICES AND GUIDING PRINCIPLES

- Sales training is a tool to translate strategy into focused activity. A company's success in doing this depends largely on designing training programs that respond to the question, "What should salespeople do differently to implement the sales strategy?"

- Use the organization's Customer Relationship Process to identify the training needs of salespeople and sales team members.

- Sales executives should never assume that they are providing enough information to the training staff to guide decisions about training program development. This understanding has to be confirmed. An effective way to do this is to create a dialogue among sales executives and training professionals. This dialogue should focus on:
  - How customers, competitors, products, and services are changing.
  - How sales strategies are changing to keep up with changes in the market.
  - The new roles salespeople will play to implement a sales strategy.
  - How salespeople should sell differently.

- To ensure that today's sales training supports today's strategy, look at the training program development process. Use the concepts of process management to find ways to shorten the time span between when the sales strategy is dictated and when training is implemented.

- Follow the model for strategic sales training outlined in this chapter. The only way to ensure that the training at the end of the path is consistent with the sales strategy is to ensure that all the steps in the process are executed well.

- Have a plan for systematic sales training for salespeople and sales managers in the organization. For example, whenever possible, train sales managers first, maintain managers' involvement in training salespeople, and ensure that salespeople are fully prepared; this means they must know what is expected of them and what the training will accomplish.

- Sales training is a process. As in any process, put measurements in place to ensure that each step is executed effectively.
  - Measurement at a number of points is an effective way to diagnose causes for less-than-desired outcomes, identify improvement opportunities, and assess particular competencies that should be the focus of follow-up training and reinforcement.
- Follow-up and reinforcement are absolutely critical. Salespeople will learn new behaviors in training; however, there are sometimes several weeks of "turbulence" back on the job while salespeople unlearn old habits and integrate new ones. Feedback, reinforcement, and assessment of strengths and weaknesses are ways to ensure that the training investment is made profitable. Follow-up and reinforcement are areas where many organizations—even some of the best sales organizations—can make tremendous gains.
- Ensure that the new behaviors learned in training are consistent with the organizational environment. For instance, if compensation or other reward plans are inconsistent with new behaviors, the training won't work.
- Look carefully at the trends in sales training. Determine those that are relevant to the organization.

Chapter Nine

Strategic Sales Coaching

"One of the most important roles in our organization is sales coaching. It is like being a conductor of a symphonic orchestra—without it, there would be nothing played at all."

—District sales manager, Rank Xerox (Sweden)

- What is strategic sales coaching?
- How can collaborative coaching enhance the performance of salespeople?
- What is meant by the "generation gap" between salespeople and sales coaches?
- What roles do effective sales managers fulfill?
- What are the barriers to effective sales coaching? How can sales managers overcome them?
- What are some important elements of sales coaching training?

Across industries, markets, and cultures—in North America, Europe, and Japan—there is a clear and unanimous vision of the profile of the ideal sales coach and the mission of sales coaching. There is also an astounding degree of consensus among salespeople, sales managers, and sales executives about the potential power of sales coaching: They agree that sales coaching is one of the most significant opportunities available to an organization to influence the performance of salespeople.

Yet in many sales organizations, there is a significant gap between the vision of sales coaching and the reality. Why? Because there has been no commitment to support sales coaching and to redefine the role of the field sales manager for today's business environment. In fact, sales managers at even the most successful sales organizations are missing important coaching opportunities—opportunities to translate sales strategy into everyday actions that can be carried out by the people they lead.

The leading sales organizations are constantly challenging themselves with the following questions:

- What is the profile of an ideal sales coach?
- What is the gap between the ideal and the reality?
- Why does the gap exist?

CRITICAL FACTORS IN COACHING

"On a scale of 1 to 10, sales coaching ranks an 11. It is extremely important."
—Field sales manager, Allen & Hanbury's (United Kingdom)

Coaching guides the development of a salesperson through one-on-one feedback and encouragement. Explained a vice president from Biscuiterie Nantaise (France), "Coaching can increase a salesperson's knowledge and set up the conditions necessary for self-development. It increases the self-confidence of the salesperson and creates a dialogue about performance."

According to salespeople, the best coaches don't tell salespeople what to do; they collaborate with them to achieve mutually agreed-upon goals. They use their coaching skills—combined with knowledge of the customer and the behind-the-scenes workings of the sales organization—to motivate their salespeople to seek continual improvement in their abilities. As a sales manager from American Airlines (United States) put it, "One of the factors that keeps us at the forefront of the industry is that managers are very communicative with individuals in counseling them, coaching them, and working with them." A vice president for France's Ordo predicted that in five years the top salespeople in his company will be the ones who benefited from effective sales coaching.

Coaching is a critical tool for sales organizations that are committed to building long-term customer relationships. To be effective in today's business environment, sales coaching must be:

- *Collaborative*—a joint, ongoing process in which sales managers and team members work together to achieve both short- and long-term sales goals.
- *Contemporary*—shaped by the needs of *today's* demanding customer and competitive marketplace as well as by the salesperson's individual development requirements.

COLLABORATIVE COACHING: FAREWELL TO THE AUTOCRATIC MANAGER

"The best sales coaches are respected by their people for their wide perspective."

—Sales manager, Sony Corporation (Japan)

Sales coaching is evolving in leading sales organizations, moving away from the traditional authoritarian patterns of manager-subordinate relationships and toward a more collaborative effort based on mutual respect and trust in which the salesperson and coach work together to achieve a common goal.

What does this look like in everyday life? Rather than *direct* the salesperson's actions, the best coaches help salespeople find their own solutions. "They adopt a counseling approach, letting the person talk and trying to redirect the discussion if they feel it's necessary," commented a sales manager from Iron Trades Insurance Group (United Kingdom). "The ideas that people take on board are ideas they feel are their own."

Effective sales managers collaborate with sales team members rather than "manage" in the traditional sense of the word. They use their authority wisely, encouraging team members to think independently. "A good coach gets you thinking about certain things, even if he or she knows the answers to the questions," observed a salesperson from Hewlett-Packard Company (United States). Not only do they resist dictating, they also resist taking over. The best coaches resist the temptation to step in and fix their salespeople's problems. They weigh the advantages of taking risks and learning-by-doing against the potential for lost time and opportunity.

The best coaches lead by example, rather than by fiat, according to both sales managers and salespeople. "Merely demanding results will not be accepted by subordinates," commented a vice president

Sales Coaching

A sequence of conversations and activities that provides ongoing feedback and encouragement to a salesperson or sales team member with the goal of improving that person's performance.

Strategic Sales Coaching

The use of sales coaching to achieve a sales strategy in a systematic way.

from Sony Corporation (Japan). A salesperson from Matra Communications (France) remarked, "I prefer the human contact, not just a boss-employee relationship." Said another from 3M (United Kingdom), "Sales coaches are there to help and not to direct."

The evolution of a collaborative model for sales coaching may be a partial consequence of the organizational changes wrought by the recent worldwide recessions. Many salespeople have stayed longer in their positions than they might have in the past, because of lack of opportunities elsewhere. As a result, many sales managers supervise sales representatives who are more educated and experienced than ever before. A collaborative approach to solving problems is one way to draw on the strengths of their resources. "With flatter organizations and changes in corporate culture, the most effective role for a sales manager is that of a coach, not an autocrat," observed a vice president from Xerox Corporation (United States). This is not to say that the collaborative approach doesn't benefit new salespeople; in fact, although they lack experience, there's a good chance they started their careers in less hierarchical organizations and aren't accustomed to the traditional authority structures.

The collaborative approach is not only a result of economics. Coincidentally, sales organizations have found that the partnerships they're consciously forming with their customers are increasingly mirrored in the relationships within their own walls, including the sales manager–salesperson relationship. This development, in fact, is encouraged: "Sales managers have to look at their salespeople as customers and think about their needs," observed a vice president from Scott Paper Company (United States). "You should probe to clarify and understand. Apply the customer needs model to your own salespeople."

In the best cases, sales coaching is a two-way exchange. In one instance, the coach may provide the salesperson with pointers on handling a customer's skepticism. In another, the salesperson may comment on how the coach interacted with the customer during a joint sales call.

Sales coaching focuses on sales behaviors that directly affect results. The effective coach looks for behaviors that demonstrate the salesperson's knowledge of the organization's products and services, mastery of the Customer Relationship Process, facility with critical selling skills (e.g., face-to-face selling, account planning, and negotiation), and knowledge of the customer's needs. A structured process can help to keep this focus.

A sales manager from Allen & Hanbury's (United Kingdom) describes how the sales coaching process works in that organization: "Each individual salesperson is assessed to see where skills must be improved to bring about an improvement in overall performance. There is a plan for each individual which is referred to, documented, and reviewed every time there is contact with that individual on a field visit."

As the Allen & Hanbury's example illustrates, sales coaching consists of two distinct, ongoing activities:

1. *Diagnosis,* in which the coach and salesperson jointly identify those behaviors that can be improved to better achieve the salesperson's targets and the organization's sales strategy. This may involve observing, reviewing revenue and customer feedback data, and gathering input from others in the company.

2. *Action planning,* in which the coach and salesperson jointly set goals based on their diagnosis. In action planning, the coach guides the process by which the salesperson finds solutions and creates plans to support short- and long-term changes that will lead to improved performance.

CONTEMPORARY COACHING: OVERCOMING THE GENERATION GAP

"My goal is to have every one of our salespeople developing, growing, and improving every day."

—Vice president, Scott Paper Company (United States)

A major challenge sales managers face in being effective coaches is addressing the needs of more sophisticated, better educated salespeople. As demonstrated earlier, many salespeople are staying in their jobs longer than in previous years. In addition, most top sales organizations have changed their hiring criteria for salespeople. "We will be adding levels of sophistication to the salesperson's job, looking for a higher level of individual to fill it," said a vice president from Hewlett-Packard Company (United States). "That will mean the sales manager's job will be more demanding, as a manager of more sophisticated resources."

Another challenge sales managers face is keeping themselves up-to-date about selling strategies that are effective in today's rapidly changing marketplace. Sales managers who were once sales representatives will find that their natural inclination is to coach people in the strategies that worked for them in the past. The problem is that the strategies that worked in previous years often do not work in today's marketplace. Customer expectations have changed—in some cases so radically that managers should question whether customers' current needs bear any resemblance to their needs when the managers themselves were salespeople. Much of their experience may, in fact, be irrelevant.

"In the past, the 'supersellers' climbed to the sales management level," commented a vice president from Bekaert (Belgium). "However, they are not adapted to today's selling strategy, and there is definitely a generation gap."

Salespeople need coaching that helps them meet the high expectations of *today's* customers. Customers want to work with a salesperson who is a strategic orchestrator, business consultant, and long-term ally—someone interested in the success of the customer's business as a whole, not just in selling a product. Yet the coaching many salespeople receive is too basic, and too infrequent, to help them develop, sell, and deliver the complex solutions their customers need and want.

The Power of "Transformational Leadership"

"No orders, no money." Those words, imprinted on a sign above a sales manager's desk in a commission-oriented organization, represent the reward-for-results approach often used to prod salespeople to perform.[1] Although this approach is effective in many organizations, Marvin Jolson, Alan Dubinsky, and their colleagues, writing in the *Sloan Management Review*, believe there's more to inspiring sales success than simply dangling a cash carrot. They suggest that the most successful sales organizations are headed by executives who employ a combination of *transactional* and *transformational* leadership styles—with a heavy emphasis on the transformational. Not surprisingly, many of the attributes of the transformational leadership style come into play in the sales manager's role as coach.

Transactional leaders motivate staff with bonuses and commissions and subscribe to a laissez-faire style of management. They establish specific targets for their people and then step back, intervening only if salespeople have trouble meeting them.

While independent self-starters may thrive under transactional leadership, inexperienced or less confident salespeople frequently perish without more guidance and feedback. Transformational leaders provide a more nurturing and, in most cases, motivational environment. This breed of leader is characterized by his or her charisma and ability to provide intellectual stimulation and individualized consideration.

Transformational managers' *charisma* inspires admiration, respect, and trust in team members. Just as important, these managers lead by example, continually modeling and reinforcing desirable attitudes and behaviors. They empower their good performers, and they exhibit genuine confidence in their salespeople.

Intellectual stimulation is a tool transformational managers use to help their people overcome sales barriers and achieve new levels of performance. It takes many forms, from encouraging creativity in solving old problems to introducing innovative prospecting and selling strategies and promoting ongoing education and learning.

(continued)

---

[1]Marvin A. Jolson, Alan J. Dubinsky, et al., "Transforming the Sales Force with Leadership," *Sloan Management Review* (Spring 1993), pp. 95–106.

The Power of "Transformational Leadership" (concluded)

Through *individualized consideration,* the transformational manager works hard to create strong, one-on-one relationships with each sales team member. That means focusing less on tasks, policies, administrative matters, or decision making and more on spending time with salespeople in their territories, holding private coaching sessions, analyzing call reports, and extending warmth and understanding.

What does it take to foster the transformational style of leadership? According to Jolson and his colleagues, first recruit sales personnel with transformational qualities and characteristics. Look for innovative and creative problem solvers and risk takers. An entrepreneurial spirit, courage, and strong personal convictions are also important. Second, provide training and development. "Because all individuals possess transformational skills to some degree," say the authors, "even minimal levels of these skills can be enhanced through training."

Three Roles of the Effective Sales Manager

Knowledge of today's marketplace not only enables sales managers to guide salespeople to customer-driven solutions; it helps them serve as effective role models for their people. It also earns the sales team's respect—a key ingredient, given *salespeople's* increasing sophistication and education.

Learning International's research indicates that top-performing sales managers fulfill three key roles (see Figure 9–1). As judged by their subordinates, colleagues, and managers, and by their track record for meeting or exceeding quotas, highly effective sales managers perform the actions associated with the following three roles better than do their less effective colleagues.

- As *strategist,* the sales manager utilizes knowledge of the organization's sales strategy and industry and market trends, needs, and perceptions to develop team strategies and goals that reflect a balance between attaining financial goals and satisfying

(continued)

Three Roles of the Effective Sales Manager (concluded)

customers. The sales manager ensures that others understand these goals; obtains commitment from salespeople to achieve them; and modifies strategies, processes, and activities based on the team's success at building lasting customer relationships.

In the role of strategist, the sales manager also develops and/or utilizes appropriate structures and systems to recruit sales personnel, create sales assignments, reward performance, pursue new business, and forecast and track revenue. He or she builds alliances throughout the organization; knows when to involve internal people or outside resources to solve problems; and supplies salespeople with the sales support, tools, and technology they need.

- As *communicator*, the sales manager organizes and uses information effectively, obtaining it from, and sharing it with, the sales team, management, and other groups. He or she possesses the interpersonal skills to seek a clear understanding of all communications, clarify expectations, and resolve conflict. The sales manager also utilizes basic and advanced selling, presentation, and negotiating skills to support salespeople in selling to accounts. He or she ensures that meeting time is used productively, maintains complete and accurate records, and gathers and uses feedback to improve customer relationships and internal processes.
- As *coach*, the sales manager establishes an environment for performance improvement. He or she does this by maintaining good rapport with the sales team and fostering open communication, collaboration, creativity, initiative, and appropriate risk taking. The sales manager encourages team members to seek information and resources to enhance their success with customers. He or she models professional attitudes and behaviors. The sales manager demonstrates awareness of individual differences among team members, helps salespeople establish clear priorities, and gives appropriate rewards and recognition.

In the role of coach, the sales manager provides each salesperson with specific feedback on strengths and weaknesses. He or she works with each person to create and implement a developmental plan to improve performance, which includes providing ongoing training and coaching in selling skills, sales strategy, and product and market knowledge.

FIGURE 9–1
The Effective Sales Manager

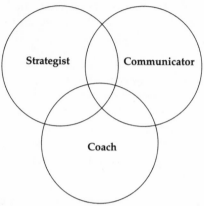

In everyday practice, the three roles overlap to some degree. When a sales manager explains the organization's marketing strategy to the sales team, for example, he or she fulfills two roles—strategist and communicator. When the manager meets with a salesperson to discuss how the organization's new product development strategy will affect his or her approach to a specific account, the sales manager is acting as both strategist and coach. These examples also illustrate that in almost all instances where the sales manager fulfills the strategist or coach role, he or she also fulfills the role of communicator.

To ensure that coaching is relevant, sales organizations need to guarantee that their coaches have current knowledge about their customers, competitors, products, and services. At Scott Paper Company (United States), for example, field sales managers have their own accounts to ensure that their selling strategies are contemporary. "We think that's really important in staying connected to customers' needs," said a Scott vice president.

BREAKING DOWN THE BARRIERS

"For best results, coaching must be a structured process. It cannot be left up to the individual manager."

—Sales manager, Océ (The Netherlands)

Pressured by short-term needs to achieve revenue targets and performance goals, many sales organizations have difficulty putting a value on the long-term benefits of sales coaching. Managers, and salespeople, naturally focus on the activities for which they are directly rewarded and compensated.

Sales coaching, however, is an essential factor in ensuring progress toward long-term goals that is consistent with the sales strategy, day by day in front of customers. Effective coaching is a steady process designed to improve salespeople's selling skills and abilities progressively over the months and years of their careers in sales. It builds on the knowledge, skills, and attitudes that salespeople learn in sales training. Sales coaching also draws on a powerful existing resource: the experienced base of sales managers.

In organizations where coaching is supported by the sales vice presidents and directors, it is a powerful tool for translating a sales strategy into everyday action. For the vast majority of other organizations, however, coaching's benefits remain unrealized.

Senior executives can play a key role in tapping the tremendous power of sales coaching. To do this, they need to understand how sales coaching can contribute to the overall sales strategy and how they will support the coaching effort. To ensure the success of the coaching process, senior executives need to change the ways that sales managers are selected, trained, motivated, and compensated.

Among organizations where sales coaching is effective, the following actions are taken:

1. *Sales managers understand that sales coaching is a priority because it supports the organization's strategy for winning and keeping customers over the long* and *short term.* There are many ways to do this, some of them very simple. For example, sales managers from Allen & Hanbury's have "learning contracts" with their manager, who periodically observes the managers at work with their salespeople. Sales managers are also required to send copies of their field visit reports to the national sales manager.

2. *Everyone has the same expectations of sales coaching.* Learning International's research indicated a wide variation among what sales managers, salespeople, senior sales executives, and even trainers believed a realistic coaching plan to be. With an agreed-upon definition, such as the one provided at the beginning of this chapter, sales coaches and salespeople can more easily set priorities and establish an effective game plan for improving the salesperson's interactions with customers. In addition, others in

the organization, such as senior management and training decision makers, will know how to channel their resources to support each salesperson's performance improvement.

3. *Coaches are trained according to their organization's definition of coaching.* A definition that is understood and accepted throughout the sales organization will provide clear direction toward the training that coaches need to be effective. The resulting training strategy can alleviate conflicting perceptions about how much coaching is occurring or about whether the coaching is actually useful to salespeople in their interactions with customers.

4. *All salespeople receive coaching.* Fast-changing market dynamics and new sales objectives make it imperative to provide coaching to all salespeople, not just to the new, inexperienced, or poor performers. Even if the sales manager cannot provide the coaching, he or she should select and train someone who can, be it another salesperson or someone hired specifically for the job.

5. *Coaches receive continuing education in market, industry, and product knowledge so they can apply leading-edge information and thinking to the situations their salespeople encounter in today's selling environment.* Of particular importance is that coaches understand the realities of today's customers and are able to guide their people in addressing them.

6. *Coaches are involved in setting objectives for training programs.* By turning to the coaches to help set objectives for training programs and even participate in their delivery, organizations can ensure that they align their sales training with current sales strategy. Coaches, in turn, will be able to build on this training in their one-on-one coaching sessions with salespeople.

7. *Others in the organization also coach.* Sales managers are the obvious choice to coach salespeople on a consistent basis, but others, such as senior sales executives and business managers, can provide key input into how best to meet customer needs. Dividing up the responsibility in this way also enables the organization to provide its salespeople with critical support without incurring additional cost or taking sales managers away from other activities that they need to address. As more organizations work in sales teams, coaching from team members is increasing.

Coaching Guidance from Several Sources

Salespeople both welcome and value coaching from their peers, training managers, business managers, technical experts, and even customers. "Your peers are your best coaches," said a salesperson from Northwestern Mutual Life Insurance Company (United States). "They are people you can trust, that know what you're doing." A salesperson from Boehme (Germany) commented, "Feedback comes from customers in the form of compliments, contracts, and sales."

"In the future," commented a vice president from Océ (The Netherlands), "not all coaching will be done by sales managers; some will be provided by technical specialists." A sales manager at Fuji Xerox (Japan) agrees: "Sales organizations will have to stretch themselves and explore new options."

TRAINING FOR COLLABORATIVE AND CONTEMPORARY COACHING

Given the complexity of today's selling challenges, it is clear that sales coaches need more than an inborn talent for being "good with people." Training in interpersonal communication skills that enable them to develop salespeople's ability to achieve the organization's financial and customer satisfaction goals is essential. Too often, however, the sales coach's own experience is thought to be an adequate source of sales wisdom, improvement strategies, and motivation.

The belief that sales coaching will happen naturally may explain why even some of today's top sales organizations have not implemented a training plan in specific sales coaching skills. In some organizations, a combination of management instruction and advanced sales training comprises the curriculum.

Not surprisingly, these organizations are not satisfied with their efforts to prepare sales managers for their coaching responsibilities. In fact, improving the competence of sales coaches appeared at the top of the list of most companies' strategies for ensuring their salespeople's success in the next 5 to 10 years.

Some organizations have taken steps to realize their beliefs about the importance of coaching. These actions range from hiring a development manager for their sales organizations, to

The Coaching Payoff: Wm. Wrigley Jr. Company

Coaching can increase an organization's success with customers, protect its sales training investments, and unify the sales force around common strategic and developmental objectives.

The Wm. Wrigley Jr. Company (United States), for example, has made coaching an integral part of its sales force training strategy. The chewing gum manufacturer started by creating task forces to define what, exactly, its salespeople and regional sales managers needed to do to ensure salespeople's success with customers. The task forces, which included managers and sales representatives from across the country, established benchmarks for salesperson performance to enable the company's regional managers to know exactly what areas to coach on—and when, why, and how.

"At one time, when our sales representatives left our training sessions and went out in the field, we had no idea how the skills were being reinforced," says one of Wrigley's division managers. "Depending on the skills and experience of the manager, one representative might receive coaching in setting up displays, another on improving selling skills. Now we have a development process based on benchmarks for successive stages in a salesperson's career.

"The process includes training the salespeople and the sales managers in critical skills, so the sales managers are able to identify their salespeople's strengths and weaknesses. As a result, our managers should be able to assess which stage their people are in and what skills they should have mastered. They'll also have the confidence, knowledge, and tools to coach their people effectively."

Hurlburt acknowledges the strategy would not be working as well if it were not for senior management involvement. "If senior management simply went along with a plan like this and didn't get involved, then our field people would think that *their* participation at less than 100 percent was also acceptable."[2]

As these actions demonstrate, Wm. Wrigley Jr. believes effective sales coaching is one vehicle that enables them to maximize their sales organization's performance with customers.

---

[2]Learning International, *Sales Coaching: The Key to Leading a High Performance Sales Team* (1994).

implementing training in sales coaching, to spelling out a schedule for their sales managers' coaching activities. The principle underlying all these actions is a commitment to ensure that their sales managers accomplish the following:

1. Establish a developmental climate based on collaboration and action in which continuous performance improvement is both encouraged and rewarded.

2. Identify for salespeople the desired performance outcomes that will achieve the organization's short- *and* long-term goals.

3. Create individual performance improvement plans that address the unique developmental needs of each sales team member.

4. Encourage and reward salespeople who achieve their developmental goals.

A comprehensive training strategy for sales coaches should include the same training that the salespeople experience. Through coaching training, sales managers come to understand not only the skills their salespeople have mastered in their own training but how to use the coaching process to build those skills and support the organization's overall sales strategy. They acquire a distinct set of interpersonal skills to diagnose each salesperson's skill development needs and to create plans to address them. They also learn how to *observe* sales interactions, not just participate in them.

Without adequate and appropriate training for sales managers, sales coaching will remain a disorganized and underutilized tool. With training, sales coaching is far more likely to yield positive results—for both the selling organization and its customers.

CONCLUSION

"Coaching rekindles the fire."

—Sales manager, Ordo (France)

Removing the obstacles to effective sales coaching isn't easy. If it were, every organization would already provide salespeople with the coaching they need. But in today's marketplace, coaching is no longer a "wish-list item." It's crucial, not only for poor performers but also for the most effective. A vice president from Iron Trades Insurance Group (United Kingdom) feels that ". . . unless sales coaching is done, and done well throughout the sales organization, then our high standards will drop." Organizations that implement a sales coaching process are far better able to achieve both their profitability and their customer satisfaction goals. In fact, they gain a substantial competitive advantage because they have made a commitment to ensuring that their salespeople's daily selling behaviors lead to mutually beneficial business relationships with customers.

BEST PRACTICES AND GUIDING PRINCIPLES

- Start with a demonstrated commitment to sales coaching by creating a developmental climate that fosters:
  - Collaboration, action, and continuous improvement.
  - Shared understanding of salesperson performance outcomes that will achieve both short- and long-term goals.
  - Development of individual performance improvement plans.
  - Behavior change.
- Ensure that senior executives and all members of the sales organization can answer these questions accurately:
  - What are the sales organization's expectations for sales coaching? How will it work?
  - How can sales coaching contribute to the organization's strategy for winning and keeping customers over the short and long term?
- Have senior executives provide visible support for sales coaching.
- Ensure that sales coaching training is consistent with the company's definition of coaching.
- Put a structured approach to sales coaching in place. Don't leave the approach completely up to the individual.
- Involve both sales managers and salespeople in the design and implementation of sales coaching programs, as well as sales staff development programs.

- Provide sales coaching to every salesperson, regardless of tenure or performance level. Tailor sales coaching to individual salespeople.
- Ensure that all sales coaches:
  - Receive continuing education to improve market, industry, and product knowledge.
  - Maintain involvement in sales staff developmental programs.
- Seek out and develop sales managers who:
  - Have a broad scope of knowledge.
  - Are able to provide inspiration and intellectual stimulation.
  - Are considerate of individuals' needs.
- Utilize a variety of people, such as peers and technical experts, in sales coaching, not just the salesperson's manager.
- Focus sales coaching on knowledge and skills that support the sales strategy. The foundation should be:
  - Knowledge of the organization's products and services.
  - Customers' needs and expectations.
  - Mastery of the company's Customer Relationship Process.
- Sales coaching should be:
  - Collaborative—a two-way exchange involving the input of both salespeople and sales managers.
  - Contemporary—grounded in the needs of today's, not yesterday's, markets and customers.
- Sales coaching training should focus on interpersonal skills, diagnosis and action-planning, and sales call observation. Sales managers should also receive continuing education to maintain current market, industry, and product knowledge.
- Sales managers should collect sufficient information about the performance of salespeople to be able to diagnose improvement needs and work with the salesperson to develop an action plan.
- Sales managers should understand the importance of fulfilling the three roles (strategist, communicator, and coach) as well as the characteristics of each.
- Sales managers should treat salespeople as customers (for instance, continually think about their needs).

Epilogue

The Next Wave

"Sales organizations need to stretch themselves to explore new options when they are faced with a situation they cannot handle through conventional wisdom. No one can foresee the future. What we can do is to build a hypothesis and act on it."

Ultimately, a sales organization's role is to translate the company's strategy from a boardroom vision to an everyday reality, add value for customers beyond that provided by the products and services, create competitive differentiation, and contribute to the company's profitability. This is a difficult mission, especially since what customers value today is very different from what they valued yesterday.

Sales organizations around the globe are all facing this challenge or a variation of this theme. Whether they sell biscuits or steel cables, they are struggling with the realities of exploding competition as well as customers who are more demanding, have more complex problems, and find it difficult to distinguish among suppliers.

This struggle is forcing sales organizations to move more quickly, be more innovative, and throw some old habits and assumptions about business relationships overboard. Traditional styles of selling and traditional roles of sales professionals are *crumbling* under the competitive pressure. Rising from the rubble is a more complex, consultative style of selling—focused on customers' strategic needs and a commitment to help customers meet *their* customers' needs better.

In every market and every industry, we saw examples of the following:

- More knowledgeable, skilled, creative, and professional sales forces, who are intensely involved in the customer's business.

- The gradual disappearance of the "lone ranger" salesperson and the advent of team selling and self-directed sales teams.
- A shift in the nature of personal and organizational relationships.
- The changing role of sales managers, from administrators and controllers to coaches and empowerers.

Although some of these trends have been evolving for years, especially in more mature industries and markets, the pace and intensity of these changes have reached record levels, and the passion with which sales professionals and customers around the world express them is astounding.

We are on the brink of major changes in the way sales organizations are managed and sales productivity is achieved. Beyond those we've discussed in this book, there are other waves of change, just emerging on the horizon, that may become important to sales organizations in the future. The following are some challenges that sales organizations are just beginning to grapple with:

1. *A new breed of salesperson.* For years, companies have had face-to-face salespeople, telemarketers, or both. But as the cost of face-to-face sales calls continues to escalate, many organizations are increasing their telesales and telemarketing activities or using other alternate channels of distribution to address the needs of specific segments of their business. They are assigning their face-to-face sales force only to segments where targeted profit margins can be achieved. Salespeople in these different channels share a core set of competencies, but each type of selling also requires competencies that are unique. As digital video and audio technology make video calling widely available, we will see the emergence of the *screen-to-screen* salesperson. This person will be a hybrid of the face-to-face and telephone salesperson, requiring the competencies of both.

2. *Re-engineering the sales force.* As suggested earlier in this book, some companies are using process management principles, benchmarking, and measurement to bring consistency to the activities the sales force performs. Some companies, such as IBM, are quite literally "going back to the drawing board," ignoring the way things *have* been done, and redesigning

them—from bottom to top—as they *should* be done. This takes tremendous vision and leadership since it means breaking apart departmental structures, reforming work relationships, creating new roles, breaking old well-entrenched habits, killing off "sacred cows," and facing changes in the market head on.

3. *Empowerment of the sales force.* Customers are asking sales organizations to give salespeople more and more decision-making authority so that they can offer customers quicker decisions. This will be supported by increased access to more information and the existence of sales teams.

4. *The "virtual" office.* Advances in technology are making it possible for sales organizations to decrease office space set aside for salespeople. Cellular phones, personal digital assistants, laptop computers, voice-mail, company databases on CD-ROM, electronic mail, fax machines, and more sophisticated project management software make it possible for the salesperson to carry his or her office around in a briefcase and yet have more product knowledge available than ever before. The result? The salesperson has a "virtual" office anywhere. Sales organizations are encouraging this. Why? To reduce the company's cost of office space and use the salesperson's time more efficiently.

5. *Sales teams.* Sales organizations are looking for alternatives to traditional reporting relationships. One emerging idea is self-directed sales teams. The goal is to allow sales organizations to react faster by minimizing communications lags, giving salespeople quicker access to information, and granting them more autonomy. In some organizations, the sales managers have been eliminated and the self-directed team fulfills those roles.

6. *Globalization.* Not so long ago, customers' expectations and suppliers' capabilities were quite different from country to country; however, they are becoming increasingly similar. We are witnessing the dawn of a shared "business culture" around the world. One of the hallmarks of this new culture is a common language that transcends differences among local markets. What is the driving force breaking down the barriers between social cultures? It is the search for, and dissemination of, best practices across borders.

The ideas in this book are topics of intense discussion in leading sales organizations around the world—and, in fact, in many other organizations as well. What distinguishes the leaders from the others are these factors:

- They're very clear about what they want to accomplish.
- They're transforming their operations systematically.
- They're experimenting with ideas and practices—including the ones discussed in this book—while other sales organizations are merely talking about them.

We find all this very encouraging. Why? First, it shows that with clear vision, unshakable commitment, discipline, determination, and willingness to take risks, great successes can be achieved. Second, *any* sales organization that has a core of bright, talented people can use some of the ideas and practices described in this book to help attain its strategic objectives.

Some of the ideas and best practices will lose popularity and disappear. Others will gain momentum, develop a following, and create nothing less than revolutions in the way sales organizations operate in the years to come.

APPENDIXES

Profile of Sales Leadership Research

SALES LEADERSHIP RESEARCH (1991–1994)

Learning International's global Sales Leadership research profiled leading sales organizations in North America, Europe, and Japan. It focused on how customer's expectations and perceptions are changing as well as how outstanding sales organizations are meeting those expectations. The study involved 300 senior sales executives, sales training managers, field sales managers, salespeople, and customers of 24 organizations. A pilot study was conducted with 11 sales organizations in Belgium and The Netherlands. Comments made by research participants appear throughout this book.

In each of the companies selected to participate in the study (see Table A–1), we interviewed sales vice presidents, sales directors, field sales managers, salespeople, sales training directors, and customers of their organizations. The interview questions explored topics such as:

- How are customers changing? How are their challenges, needs, and expectations evolving? What is influencing these changes?
- How is the competitive environment changing? Why is it getting continually harder to maintain a competitive edge?
- What sales strategies are leading sales organizations implementing?
- How will salespeople have to sell differently in the coming decade?
- What do leading sales organizations do to ensure that their salespeople are successful in a changing market?

TABLE A–1
Companies Participating in the Sales Leadership Research[1]

Market	Company	Industry
North America	United States	
	American Airlines	Transportation services
	Hewlett-Packard Company	Computers/high technology
	Northwestern Mutual Life Insurance Company	Insurance
	Scott Paper Company	Paper/forest products
	Xerox Corporation	Office equipment
Europe	France	
	Biscuiterie Nantaise	Foods
	Matra-Hachette	Telecommunications
	Ordo	General manufacturing
	Germany	
	Bayerische Vereinsbank	Financial services
	Boehme Chemie	Health and beauty aids
	Siemens	Semiconductors/electronics
	Belgium	
	N.V. Bekaert	Steel production
	The Netherlands	
	Océ van der Grinten	Office equipment
	Rank Xerox Netherlands	Office equipment
	Sweden	
	Rank Xerox Sweden	Office equipment
	United Kingdom	
	3M	Precision manufacturing
	Allen & Hanbury's	Pharmaceuticals
	Iron Trades Insurance Group	Insurance
	Rank Xerox	Office equipment
Pacific Rim	Japan	
	Fuji Xerox Company	Office equipment
	NEC Corporation	Electronics/semiconductors
	Sony Corporation	Electronics/semiconductors
	Shiseido Corporation	Cosmetics
	Tokio Marine & Fire Insurance Company	Financial services

[1]The North American companies were recognized by *Sales & Marketing Management* magazine as top performers. The European and Japanese companies were selected because of their extraordinary sales performance and reputation in their local markets.

- How can training, coaching, process and management enhance the performance of salespeople?
- What attitudes, skills, knowledge, and personal characteristics typify the most outstanding salespeople and sales managers in these companies?

By asking each group similar questions, we were able to capture a variety of points of view. We also interviewed customers who deal with each company to understand the extent to which sales leaders are meeting their expectations and to understand what customers like—and dislike—about salespeople and sales organizations.

COMPANY PROFILES

Allen & Hanbury's (United Kingdom)

Allen & Hanbury's is a manufacturer of pharmaceuticals located in Middlesex, England. It is owned by Glaxo Holdings, the second largest pharmaceutical manufacturer in the world, with 1993 worldwide sales of $5.0 billion.*

American Airlines (United States)

American Airlines has the highest revenues of any airline and has been rated best in service among all U.S. carriers. A subsidiary of the AMR Corporation, American Airlines has expanded during the last few years using acquisitions and marketing alliances to develop a stronger international route network. In 1993, operating income was $14.7 billion.

Bayerische Vereinsbank Groupe (Germany)

Bayerische Vereinsbank Groupe is a market-oriented bank based in Munich, Germany. In 1992, they recorded total assets at approximately DM 251 billion, or $147.5 billion.

---

*All financial data are presented in U.S. dollars.

N.V. Bekaert S.A. (Belgium)

Bekaert, founded in 1880 and located in Kortrijk, Belgium, is a manufacturer of steel, steel wire and steel wire products, and steel cord. They are also involved in engineering and consulting. Sales in 1992 reached approximately BF 53 billion or $1.6 billion.

Biscuiterie Nantaise (France)

Biscuiterie Nantaise, headquartered in Nantes, France, is a well-established company that manufactures a wide variety of cookies, biscuits, and snacks. It is now a joint venture between U.S.–based Pepsico Foods International, which registered $25 billion in sales in 1993, and General Mills, Inc., with $8.5 billion in sales in 1994. BN is the leader in the markets for gouterfourrés cookies and salted snacks and is known for its innovative products and marketing.

Boehme Chemie Gesellschaft (Germany)

Boehme Chemie Gesellschaft, headquartered in Dusseldorf, Germany, produces and distributes detergents and organic and inorganic chemicals such as soap powders, fabric softeners, starches, car care products, adhesives, cosmetics, insecticides, and herbicides. Boehme Chemie is owned by Henkel KGAA, whose sales in 1992 reached $3.2 billion.

Fuji Xerox Company, Ltd. (Japan)

Fuji Xerox, based in Tokyo, Japan, manufactures and markets xerographic copiers and duplicators, and other office equipment. Jointly owned by Rank Xerox Ltd. and Fuji Photo Film Company Ltd., Fuji Xerox recorded 1993 sales at approximately ¥ 571.9 billion.

Hewlett-Packard Company (United States)

Hewlett-Packard is the world's largest and most diversified manufacturer of electronic measurement and testing equipment and the world's second largest computer workstation manufacturer. Hewlett-Packard, a Palo Alto, California–based firm, offers products which include reduced-instruction-set computing (RISC) minicomputers and computer workstations, networking products, medical electronic equipment, testing and measurement systems, calculators, and chemical analysis systems. In 1993, sales reached $20.3 billion.

Iron Trades Insurance Group (United Kingdom)

Iron Trades Insurance Group is a leading provider of all classes of insurance policy and underwriting services to personal buyers and commercial sectors, via a well-developed network of offices throughout the United Kingdom. Headquartered in London, the company is privately held.

Matra-Hachette (France)

Matra-Hachette is a manufacturer of high-technology communications products. It is a division of Matra S.A., which is a Paris-based defense manufacturer focusing on products such as airborne and land-based weapons, space telecommunications, electronic components, robotics, motor vehicles, and automated urban and interurban transport systems. In 1993, Matra merged with Hachette, creating a new company called Matra-Hachette. In 1992, sales were estimated at FF 55 billion. Matra-Hachette is a subsidiary of Lagardere Groupe holding company.

Minnesota Mining & Manufacturing (3M) (United Kingdom)

Minnesota Mining & Manufacturing (3M) is a distributor of tape and adhesive products, electronic connectors and devices, surgical and medical supplies, and pharmaceutical and consumer products. The parent company, located in St. Paul, Minnesota, recorded net sales for 1993 at $14.0 billion with approximate sales at $13 billion. The United Kingdom division is headquartered in Berkshire, England.

NEC Corporation (Japan)

NEC is an international supplier of communications systems and equipment, computers, and industrial electronic systems and electron devices. Revenue in 1993 was $30.6 billlion or ¥ 3.5 trillion.

Northwestern Mutual Life Insurance Company (United States)

Northwestern Mutual is the 10th largest life insurance company in the United States, with assets of $44 billion (1993). The Milwaukee, Wisconsin–based company has more than 2 million policyholders of life and disability insurance and annuities. Northwestern has 4.1 million policies, with more than $224 billion of insurance in force. Northwestern markets its services through a nationwide network of 7,200 exclusive agents and operates in all 50 U.S. states and the District of Columbia, with more than 100 general agency offices.

Océ van der Grinten, N.V. (Netherlands)

Océ, founded in 1877 and based in The Netherlands, produces and sells printers and printer supplies, plain-paper copiers, plotters, and overhead films. In 1993, net sales were approximately NG 2.6 billion.

Ordo S.A. (France)

Ordo is the largest manufacturer and distributor of wooden office furniture in France, with 23 percent of the market. Ordo, a French company, was created in 1910 and run by a cabinet maker, Rene Leveque. Nearly 70 percent of Ordo's employees are cabinet makers. In 1992, Ordo became part of the Haworth Group (United States). Ordo's sales in 1992 were approximately FF 204 million.

Rank Xerox (United Kingdom)

Rank Xerox, based in Buckinghamshire, England, is jointly owned by Xerox Corporation and the Rank Organization of the United Kingdom. Benefitting from both Xerox, who manufactures reprographic and electronic printing systems, and Rank, who manufactures consumer and industrial scientific and electronic equipment, Rank Xerox delivers a full range of Document Processing products and services to 80 countries in Europe, Africa, the Middle East, and Asia. Sales in 1992 were registered at £1.9 billion or $3.2 billion.

Scott Paper Company (United States)

Scott Paper Company, located in Philadelphia, Pennsylvania, is the world's leading manufacturer of tissue products, such as toilet paper and paper towels, and one of America's leading producers of coated printing and publishing papers. Scott's commercial division has substantial sales in paper towel systems, cloth replacement wipes, and cleaners. Scott Paper sells its paper and nonwoven fiber products in more than 60 countries, and most of its foreign operations are at least 50 percent locally owned. The commercial division participated in Learning International's study. Scott's 1993 sales totaled $4.7 billion.

Shiseido Company (Japan)

Shiseido Company, a Tokyo, Japan–based firm, is a major manufacturer and exporter of cosmetics and toiletries. Divisions and subsidiaries include Carita, Beaute Prestige International (BPI), Alma Coiffure, and Zotos International. Sales in 1991 reached $3.5 billion, with approximately 16 percent coming from exports.

Siemens (Germany)

Siemens, headquartered in Munich, Germany, develops, manufactures, sells, and services a wide range of systems and products related to the production, distribution , and application of electricity. Uses include power generation, power transmission and distribution, private and public communication systems, defense electronics, and audio and video systems. In 1993, revenues were DM 81.6 billion.

Sony Corporation (Japan)

Sony Corporation, based in Tokyo, Japan, is a world leader in consumer electronics, video technology, recordings, and films, generating approximately 70 percent of its sales outside of Japan. Sony also owns 52.5 percent of audio equipment manufacturer Aiwa. Sony's new hardware technologies include high-definition television and 8-mm video. Net sales in 1993 reached $34.4 billion or ¥ 3.9 trillion.

The Tokio Marine & Fire Insurance Company (Japan)

The Tokio Marine & Fire Insurance Company is the world's largest property and casualty insurance company. Japan's property and casualty insurance market is the second largest in the world, after the United States. Through a domestic network of 529 offices, the company provides marine, fire, casualty, and auto insurance. Assets in 1993 totaled ¥ 6.8 trillion or $58.9 billion.

Xerox Corporation (United States)

Xerox is the world's leading manufacturer of high-end copiers. The company also makes scanners, printers, and document processing software. Xerox The Document Company is committed to redefining the way information, whether in paper or electronic form, moves through corporate offices. Xerox was a 1989 Malcolm Baldrige Award winner. Sales in 1993 were recorded at $16.8 billion.

COMPANIES THAT PARTICIPATED IN THE PILOT PHASE

Following are the eleven companies that participated in the Benelux pilot study:

Name	Industry
Artic	Frozen foods
Avis Fleet Services	Auto fleet leasing
BP Oil International	Petrochemicals
N.V. Bekaert	Steel wire and cord
Gregg	Temporary office services
KN Nederland	Office equipment
Océ	Office equipment
Philip Morris	Cigarettes/tobacco
Schering	Pharmaceuticals
TNT	Air transport
Veldhoven Beheermaatschappij	Textile/apparel

Sales Performance Research Studies from Learning International

For information about the research cited in this appendix, contact the following offices:

In North America

Learning International
225 High Ridge Road
P.O. Box 10211
Stamford, CT 06904
United States
Telephone: (800) 456-9390
or (203) 965-8677

In Canada

Learning International
207 Queen's Quay West
Box 140, Suite 890
Toronto, Ontario M5J 1A7
Canada
Telephone: (800) 668-2168
or (416) 203-5858

In Europe

Learning International
250 Gunnersbury Ave.
Chiswick, London W4 5QB
United Kingdom
Telephone: (44 81) 994-8592

In Asia

Learning International
c/o Times Mirror Singapore
#09-04 Forum
583 Orchard Rd.
Singapore 0923
Telephone: (65) 737-2095

SALES LEADERSHIP RESEARCH (1991–1994)

Learning International's global Sales Leadership research, an international study of leading sales organizations in North America, Europe, and Japan, focused on how customers' expectations and perceptions are changing as well as how outstanding sales organizations around the world are meeting those expectations. The study involved 300 senior sales executives, sales training managers, field sales managers, salespeople, and customers of 24 organizations. A pilot study was conducted with 11 sales organizations in Belgium and The Netherlands. The research revealed that sales organizations are employing a variety of different sales strategies to develop long-term relationships with customers and adapt to changes in their markets. Aspects of the research were incorporated into the white paper *Sales Coaching: The Key to Leading a High-Performance Sales Team.* Comments made by research participants appear throughout this book.

ROLES OF THE SALESPERSON (1987, 1990, 1994)

Learning International's Roles of the Salesperson research was conducted to gain an understanding of the characteristics and practices of top-performing salespeople. The two-phased study involved more than 1,600 salespeople and sales managers at 33 North American manufacturing and service companies. The research examined the behaviors that distinguish salespeople who are judged to be highly effective by colleagues and customers, as well as by their achievement of quota. It revealed that top-performing salespeople consistently fulfill three roles: strategic orchestrator, business consultant, and long-term ally.

CUSTOMER LOYALTY RESEARCH (1989, 1991–92)

This study identified the factors important to the buyer-seller relationship, with particular focus on determining why customers sever relationships with supplier organizations. Through focus groups and telephone interviews with more than 200 buyers in seven industries in North America, six factors were uncovered: Business Expertise and Image, Dedication to the Customer, Account Sensitivity and Guidance, Product Performance and Quality, Service Department Excellence, and Confirmation of Capabilities. The first three have the greatest impact on overall customer satisfaction and rely heavily on the salesperson's skill and involvement before, during, and after the sale, highlighting the pivotal role a salesperson plays in building customer loyalty. This research served as the basis for the *Profiles in Customer Loyalty* white paper.

After the North American study was conducted, the research was replicated in 12 countries in North America, Europe, and the Pacific Rim in 1991 and 1992. The European research served as the basis for the white paper *Achieving Customer Loyalty in Europe*.

SALES PRODUCTIVITY (1990)

In 1990, Learning International conducted research to identify the management activities that have the most critical effect on sales productivity. Information was gathered through telephone interviews with 300 sales executives in a variety of industries as well as through focus groups with sales executives in U.S. and Canadian companies. Although 10 activities were identified as having a major effect on sales productivity, the following three activities have the greatest impact: building long-term relationships with clients, providing salespeople with in-depth knowledge of the company's products or services, and maintaining a positive image of their organization in the marketplace. This study served as the basis for the white paper *Sales Productivity Action Planning Guide*.

SERVICE EXCELLENCE (1990)

The Service Excellence research examined the philosophies, strategies, and service employee competencies that characterize top service organizations. Interviews were conducted with front-line service employees, service managers, general managers, and customers in 14 U.S. companies recognized for their focus on providing outstanding customer service. Based on these interviews, Learning International identified several common philosophies and practices that foster superior customer relations: collecting feedback from customers to assess their needs, empowering front-line service employees to better serve the customer, emphasizing continuous service improvement, and involving senior managers in customer service. In addition, the study determined that service-minded organizations hire, develop, and motivate their service personnel to be skilled in 15 "master competencies," ranging from building customer loyalty and confidence to using effective inter-personal skills. This research served as the basis for the *Lessons from Top Service Providers* white paper.

SALES FORCE TURNOVER (1989)

This study examined sales force turnover in an effort to identify the reasons salespeople leave their jobs and to assess what managers can do to improve sales force retention. Conducted through telephone interviews with 337 sales managers and 165 salespeople selected randomly from major U.S. and Canadian firms, the research revealed that sales force turnover occurred at an annual rate of approximately 27 percent, costing the average company up to $200,000. A key finding of the study was that high sales force turnover can be avoided through a systematic management strategy to provide salespeople with the fundamentals they need to perform their jobs effectively. This study served as the basis for the white paper *What Does Sales Force Turnover Cost You?*

ROLES OF THE SALES MANAGER (1987)

This study identified the critical behaviors of effective sales managers, based on 2,500 written questionnaires completed by 187 managers and selected colleagues, subordinates, and superiors in 20 private and public North American organizations. The research revealed that sales managers can improve their productivity by developing their ability in three key roles: strategist, communicator, and mentor. In addition, highly effective sales managers must consistently fulfill all three roles. This research served as the basis for Learning International's *Challenges of Sales Management* program.

SALES AND MARKETING TRENDS (1987)

A 1987 study of sales and marketing trends commissioned by Learning International identified key factors that have an impact on the sales function in 10 high-growth industries. Interviews with 135 senior sales and marketing executives from 80 organizations revealed the 10 key trends that affect the sales environment: increasing competition; consolidated buying groups; broader, more diverse product/service lines; technological breakthroughs; elongated sales cycles; shortened product life cycles; increasing customer sophistication; service orientation; deregulation; and customer demand–driven selling environment. These research findings were confirmed in a 1989 follow-up study conducted in the high-technology and financial service industries.

Appendix C

Customer Loyalty Research

Learning International's Customer Loyalty research identified the factors important to the buyer-seller relationship, with particular focus on determining why customers sever relationships with supplier organizations. The same expectations ranked as the top 10 in three markets—North America, Europe, and Japan. The complete list of expectations is shown here.

A product or service that:

Is priced competitively.
Has a high level of technical support.
Has support in product application/usage.
Allows purchasing specific features.
Is delivered on time.
Performs as anticipated.
Is compatible with products and services purchased.
Is not quickly obsolete.

A salesperson who:

Knows his or her competition.
Wants business.
Brings in others to meet needs.
Is honest.
Has a pleasant personality.
Helps customer solve problems.
Knows his or her products and services.

Is backed by his or her own company.
Provides a total package.
Helps the customer be successful.
Anticipates problems.
Suggests creative solutions.
Provides guidance.
Instills confidence.
Presents products understandably.
Meets customers' emergency needs.
Keeps promises.
Takes a long-term perspective.
Helps sell recommendations.
Lets the customer know of changes.
Has a good personal appearance.
Can be reached when needed.
Responds to customer concerns.
Acknowledges product/service weaknesses.
Understands business and economic trends.
Understands decision-making process.
Helps the customer provide better products and services.
Works to develop a smarter way of doing business.

A supplier organization that:

Has a name recognized in the marketplace.
Has a good reputation in the marketplace.
Projects awareness of social responsibility.
Is associated with high-quality products and services.
Has high-caliber management.
Is financially stable.
Has been in business for a long time.
Is associated with innovation.
Adapts to changes in the marketplace.
Allows on-site inspection.
Provides customer references.
Can be trusted.

Customer service providers who:

Are sensitive to the customer's needs.

Have the customer's best interest in mind.

Are dependable.

Ask appropriate questions for information.

Pay attention to what the customer says.

Are always willing to help.

Understand customer concerns.

Are courteous.

Are knowledgeable.

Indicate plans to help the customer.

Explain when services will be performed.

Provide prompt service.

Are easily accessible.

Solve customers' problems.

Make the customer feel confident in business dealings.

The Consultative Salesperson: Knowledge, Skills, Attitudes, and Personal Characteristics

This appendix lists the knowledge, skills, attitudes, and personal characteristics necessary for conducting the practices associated with the roles of strategic orchestrator, business consultant, and long-term ally. A needs analysis within your own organization would reveal which of these are most important for your business.

Knowledge of:

- Your company's products and services.

    Applications.

    How they can be combined to best meet your customer's needs.

- Competitive products and services.

    Communicates the advantages and disadvantages.

    How they compare with your own products and services.

    Under what conditions they might be recommended.

- General business knowledge.

    How businesses work.

    General business, industry, and economic trends.

- Your company.

    Your sales strategy.

    Functions and capabilities of various departments, teams, groups, and individuals and how they can add value.

    Your company's policies and procedures.

Skills:

- Research skills.

  Uncovers the customer's business, products and services, competition, industry, culture, organization.

  Reads annual reports and other current information.

  Accesses databases.

  Identifies the customer's decision-making process.
- Communication skills.

  Listens actively.

  Demonstrates understanding.

  Expresses ideas clearly and logically.

  Probes effectively; asks insightful questions.

  Interviews people throughout the customer organization.

  Persuades.

  Gains commitment.

  Develops and delivers formal and informal presentations.

  Presents a professional image, verbally and nonverbally.

  Expresses ideas well verbally, in person, and by phone.

  Writes clearly and succinctly.
- Self management skills.

  Builds effective networks.

  Uses time and territory effectively.

  Gathers feedback, and identifies ways to be more productive.
- Problem-solving and planning skills.

  Identifies needs and challenges.

  Gathers relevant information.

  Analyzes data and draws appropriate conclusions.

  Generates creative solutions.

  Assesses alternative solutions.

  Makes decisions.

  Makes appropriate recommendations.
- Organization skills.

  Organizes information.

Performs pre-call analyses.

Prepares for sales call.

Organizes information after sales call.

- Team skills.

Identifies situations where a team approach is appropriate.

Puts together ad-hoc teams.

Delegates responsibility.

Leads teams.

Organizes activities of team members.

Tracks progress of teams.

Uses support systems.

- Financial skills.

Calculates financial impact of recommendations and various activities.

Oversees invoicing.

- Negotiation skills.

Plans for negotiations.

Negotiates solutions in which the customer, salesperson, and sales organization all win.

- Interpersonal skills.

Demonstrates appropriate humor.

Demonstrates consideration for the customer's time.

Makes others feel comfortable and important.

Is accessible; responds quickly to requests.

Credits others for ideas.

Doesn't pressure the customer.

- Maintains relationships.

Provides added-value information, ideas, and services.

Attitudes and Personal Characteristics:

- Intelligence.

Learns quickly.

Absorbs vast amounts of information.

Is able to sort out important information from unimportant information.

- Commitment.
    Continues own education and self-improvement.
    Helps the customer achieve short-term and long-term business objectives.
- Customer-focused approach.
    Does what is right for the customer.
    "Keeps an eye out" for the customer—even when not doing business.
    Stays interested.
- Proactive approach.
    Looks for opportunities instead of waiting to react.
    Is assertive; asks for business.
    Takes initiative.
    Asks for feedback.
- Credibility and integrity.
    Is honest—acknowledges limitations and admits mistakes.
    Stands up for beliefs.
    Demonstrates integrity under all circumstances.
    Only promises what the company can deliver.
    Communicates genuine interest and concern through words and actions.
    Is tactful and responsible.
    Keeps confidential information confidential.
    Never criticizes others in his or her own organization.
- Thoroughness.
    Looks after the details.
    Follows through consistently.
- Common sense.
- Reliability.
    Completes projects, and delivers things on time.
    Is prompt for appointments.
- Flexibility, adaptability.
    Alters plans, arrangements, and activities according to customers' changing needs.
    Is willing to give up preconceived notions.

- Optimism.

  Believes in the value of products and services.

  Has a winning attitude.

  Sees competition and problems as opportunities to demonstrate excellence.

  Takes competitive losses gracefully.

  Sees failure or rejection as an opportunity to learn.

- Energy level.

  Works hard.

  Constantly looks for new opportunities.

- Ambition.

  Sets challenging personal goals.

  Sets and follows a career path.

  Commits to excellence.

- Motivation.

  Sets high goals.

  Seeks nonfinancial rewards.

  Has a strong work ethic.

The Salesperson of the '90s—From the Customer's Point of View

While doing the research for this book, we had the opportunity to speak to a number of insightful customers. Listen to what they say about the knowledge, skills, attitudes, and personal characteristics of the "quintessential" salesperson:

Knowledge

"The level of competence demanded of salespeople will take quantum leaps. They need to be more professional, more clever, and have more technical knowledge because the customer base is more sophisticated about business."

—Customer, Scott Paper Company (United States)

Skills

"Salespeople should not focus on what they want to sell but must sell to the needs."

—Customer, American Airlines (United States)

"They sell from the top down; they get as high as they can in the organization to find someone who understands how the products are used and what the cost and use issues are."

—Customer, Scott Paper Company (United States)

"They think logically; they base decisions on facts and data."

—Customer, Tokio Marine & Fire Insurance Company (Japan)

"Once they understand a problem, they own it."

—Customer, American Airlines (United States)

"To be successful in sales, you need to be an intelligent listener . . . Most salespeople, however, are like alligators—they have great big mouths, little eyes, and little ears."

—Customer, Scott Paper Company (United States)

"They help me make good decisions and give me the tools to defend my decision within my company."

—Customer, Océ (The Netherlands)

"They ask questions to uncover the priorities, but it feels like a conversation in the living room with your best friend."

—Customer, Scott Paper Company (United States)

"Salespeople have to be better at everything than they used to be—more technically knowledgeable, good negotiators, good problem solvers. There is also a trend toward salespeople offering a more complete service to customers; more of an entrepreneur . . . than a salesperson."

—Customer, 3M (United Kingdom)

"If salespeople are going to grow the business, they need to be able to keep lots of balls in the air. Otherwise the business will plateau. So, good organizational skills are critical."

—Customer, Scott Paper Company (United States)

Attitudes and Personal Characteristics

"After a long negotiation, he lost out on a large deal. He took it very well, and we continued after that loss on a professional basis. This surprised me. He was a good loser, and he remained a professional."

—Customer, Océ (The Netherlands)

"They have to become broad in their vision. Stop short-term thinking and build the long-term relationship. It's crucial."

—Customer, Océ (The Netherlands)

"The salesperson must build the customer's confidence . . . find a solution in order to reassure the buyer, and prove one's good intentions.

—Customer, Matra (France)

"They must fulfill promises. Even when the company they work for doesn't keep promises, I still hold them liable."

—Customer, Océ (The Netherlands)

"You can build a house on what they promise."

—Customer, BP Oil (Benelux)

"Not sticking to your promises ends the relationship, as far as I'm concerned."

—Customer, Philip Morris (Belgium)

"Integrity is the umbrella I find crucial."

—Customer, Océ (The Netherlands)

"If there is a complaint, they listen to what you have to say, and then take action quickly."

—Customer, Iron Trades Insurance (United Kingdom)

"Have a genuine, helpful, caring attitude."

—Customer, American Airlines (United States)

"If you can't meet expectations, don't sell."

—Customer, Gregg (Benelux)

Glossary

Best practice. The best known procedures or activities that can be used to achieve a desired outcome.

Business consultant. A salesperson who fosters customer confidence and strengthens selling relationships by demonstrating:

- General business knowledge.
- A comprehensive understanding of the customer's business challenges.
- An ability to develop and help implement effective solutions and recommendations.

Consultative selling. The process of helping the customer achieve strategic goals through the use of your product or service.

Creative problem solving. The ability to develop and combine nontraditional alternatives to meet the specific needs of the situation.

Customer Relationship Process (CRP). The sequence of activities performed by the people who are in direct contact with customers that enable the supplier organization to meet or exceed customer requirements.

Ideal business relationship. A business relationship characterized by a sense of rapport, trust, and respect between the salesperson and customer, with the expectation that their organizations will do business over the long term and in a mutually beneficial way.

Long-term ally. Salesperson who demonstrates commitment—and is able to contribute—to the customer's immediate- and long-term success throughout the entire Customer Relationship Process.

Loyal customer. A buyer who chooses to do business with a particular supplier and intends to buy from that supplier in the future.

Sales coaching. A sequence of conversations and activities that provides ongoing feedback and encouragement to a salesperson or sales team member with the goal of improving that person's performance.

Sales executive. Sales vice-presidents and directors of sales.

Sales strategy. The sales organization's role in adding value, meeting customer expectations, and differentiating from competition.

Sales training. The process of providing a salesperson or sales team member with the skills, knowledge, and attitudes necessary to increase that person's productivity.

Satisfied customer. A buyer who buys from a particular supplier, but expects to buy from others in the future.

Strategic orchestrator. A salesperson who coordinates all of the information, resources, and activities needed to support customers before, during, and after the sale.

Strategic sales coaching. The use of sales coaching to achieve a sales strategy in a systematic way.

Strategic sales training. The use of sales training to achieve a sales strategy in a systematic way.

Team selling. When a team from the supplier organization meets with a potential or existing customer with the intention of advancing a sales cycle and building a business relationship.

Bibliography

Cespedes, Frank V.; Stephen X. Doyle; and Robert J. Freedman. "Teamwork for Today's Selling." *Harvard Business Review*, March/April 1989, pp. 44–58.

Fay, Christopher. "Royalties from Loyalties." *Journal of Business Strategy* 15, no. 2 (March/April 1994), pp. 47–51.

Hayes and S. W. Harley. "How Buyers View Industrial Salespeople." *Industrial Marketing Management* 18 (1989), pp. 73–80.

Herrington, Mike. "What Does a Customer Want?" *Across the Board, The Conference Board*, 1993.

Howard, James S. "Suppliers and Customers Put Down the Gloves." *D & B Reports* 41, no. 3 (May/June 1992), pp. 26–28.

Jolson, Marvin A.; Alan J. Dubinsky, et al.. "Transforming the Sales Force with Leadership." *Sloan Management Review*, Spring 1993, pp. 95–106.

Journal of Business and Industrial Marketing 8, no. 4 (1993).

King, James P. "Union Pacific Gets Back on Track with Training." *Training and Development*, August 1993, pp. 30–37.

Kirkpatrick, D. L. "Techniques for Evaluating Training Programs." *Training Director's Journal*, November 1959.

Learning International. *Achieving Customer Loyalty in Europe*. White paper, 1992.

Learning International. *Exchange*, no. 36 (1991), p. 3.

Learning International. *Profiles in Customer Loyalty*. White paper, 1989.

Learning International. *Sales Productivity Action Planning Guide*. White paper, 1992.

Learning International. "Sales Productivity in the 1990s." Preliminary report, 1990, p. 9.

Linsalata, Ralph; and Richard Highland. "Re-engineering the Selling Process." White paper. Waltham, MA: Eavoiy Systems Corporation.

O'Connell, William A.; and William Keenan, Jr. "The Shape of Things to Come." *Sales and Marketing Management Magazine*, January 1990, p. 38.

Porter, Michael E. *The Competitive Advantage of Nations*. New York: The Free Press, 1990.

Reichheld, Fredrick F. W.; and Earl Sasser, Jr. "Zero Defections: Quality Comes to Service." *Harvard Business Review*, September/October 1990.

Retchfeld, Barry. *Personal Selling Power 13*, no. 6 (September 1993), pp. 26–33.

Sager, Ira. "The Few, The True, The Blue." *Business Week*, May 30, 1994.

Stalk, George Jr. and Thomas M. Hout. *Competing Against Time*. New York: The Free Press, 1990.

Standard & Poor's Industry Surveys. *Health Care Products and Services*, September 9, 1993, p. 39.

Treacy, Michael; and Fred Wiersema. "Customer Intimacy and Other Value Disciplines." *Harvard Business Review*, January/February 1993, pp. 84–93.

Wexley, K. N.; and G. P. Lathaam. *Developing and Training Human Resources in Organizations*. New York: HarperCollins, 1991.

Index

Other books of interest to you from Irwin Professional Publishing . . .

LEADING TEAMS

Mastering the New Role

John H. Zenger, Ed Musselwhite, Kathleen Hurson, and Craig Perrin

Focuses specifically on the role of the leader as the key to long-term success.
Shows how managers can carve an enduring and vital position for themselves in
a team environment. (275 pages)
ISBN: 1-55623-894-0

SELF-DIRECTED WORK TEAMS

The New American Challenge

Jack D. Orsburn, Linda Moran, Ed Musselwhite, and John H. Zenger

Shows employees from diverse areas of a company how to work together efficiently so the organization can compete more effectively. Includes case histories
from TRW, General Electric, and many more. (354 pages)
ISBN: 1-55623-341-8

Harness These Leading-Edge Sales Strategies!

Let Learning International Help You Build—and Sustain—A Competitive Advantage

As the worldwide leader in sales and service training, Learning International is committed to helping organizations achieve competitive advantage by strengthening their effectiveness at the front lines—where customers are won or lost daily. Our unparalleled training programs can provide your organization with the skills, knowledge, and attitudes that research has shown to have the most decisive impact on performance.

To find out how Learning International can help you to increase customer loyalty and profitability, please complete and return this card or call us at **1-800-456-9390.**

Yes, I'd like to learn more . . .

❑ Please have an account executive contact me to discuss Learning International's capabilities

❑ Please send me information about Learning International's programs and services

❑ Please contact me about upcoming conferences and executive briefings

I am interested in the following types of training:

❑ Sales ❑ Sales management

❑ Service ❑ Service management

Name _____

Address _____

City _____

State _____Zip _____

Phone _____

Harness These Leading-Edge Sales Strategies!

Let Learning International Help You Build—and Sustain—A Competitive Advantage

As the worldwide leader in sales and service training, Learning International is committed to helping organizations achieve competitive advantage by strengthening their effectiveness at the front lines—where customers are won or lost daily. Our unparalleled training programs can provide your organization with the skills, knowledge, and attitudes that research has shown to have the most decisive impact on performance.

To find out how Learning International can help you to increase customer loyalty and profitability, please complete and return this card or call us at **1-800-456-9390.**

Yes, I'd like to learn more . . .

❑ Please have an account executive contact me to discuss Learning International's capabilities

❑ Please send me information about Learning International's programs and services

❑ Please contact me about upcoming conferences and executive briefings

I am interested in the following types of training:

❑ Sales ❑ Sales management

❑ Service ❑ Service management

Name _____

Address _____

City _____

State _____Zip _____

Phone _____

BUSINESS REPLY MAIL
FIRST CLASS MAIL   PERMIT No.337   STAMFORD, CT

POSTAGE WILL BE PAID BY ADDRESSEE

LEARNING INTERNATIONAL
225 High Ridge Road
P.O. Box 10211
Stamford, CT 06913-0518

BUSINESS REPLY MAIL
FIRST CLASS MAIL   PERMIT No.337   STAMFORD, CT

POSTAGE WILL BE PAID BY ADDRESSEE

LEARNING INTERNATIONAL
225 High Ridge Road
P.O. Box 10211
Stamford, CT 06913-0518